Thoreau's Pedagogy of Awakening

Thoreau's Pedagogy of Awakening

Clodomir Barros de Andrade

HAMILTON BOOKS
an imprint of
ROWMAN & LITTLEFIELD
Lanham • Boulder • New York • London

Published by Hamilton Books
An imprint of The Rowman & Littlefield Publishing Group, Inc.
4501 Forbes Boulevard, Suite 200, Lanham, Maryland 20706
www.rowman.com

86-90 Paul Street, London EC2A 4NE, United Kingdom

Copyright © 2022 by The Rowman & Littlefield Publishing Group, Inc.

All rights reserved. No part of this book may be reproduced in any form or by any electronic or mechanical means, including information storage and retrieval systems, without written permission from the publisher, except by a reviewer who may quote passages in a review.

British Library Cataloguing in Publication Information Available

Library of Congress Cataloging-in-Publication Data Available

Names: Andrade, Clodomir Barros de, author.
Title: Thoreau's pedagogy of awakening / Clodomir Barros de Andrade.
Description: Lanham : Hamilton Books, [2022] | Includes bibliographical references and index. | Summary: "This book is a poetic and philosophic meditation on Thoreau's work, highlighting his 'pedagogy of awakening,' that is, a path towards a non-dual and enlightening experience with nature"—Provided by publisher.
Identifiers: LCCN 2021058382 (print) | LCCN 2021058383 (ebook) |
  ISBN 9780761872726 (paperback) | ISBN 9780761872733 (epub)
Subjects: LCSH: Thoreau, Henry David, 1817-1862—Philosophy.
Classification: LCC PS3057.P4 D4 2022 (print) | LCC PS3057.P4 (ebook) |
  DDC 818/.309—dc23/eng/20211209
LC record available at https://lccn.loc.gov/2021058382
LC ebook record available at https://lccn.loc.gov/2021058383

To my parents, Eduardo and Vaina

Contents

Acknowledgments	ix
Introduction	1
1 Concord, Cosmos	19
2 The Long Shadow of Prometheus: Civilization and Alienation	37
3 Sacramental Technique	55
4 Being Wild: Thoreau's pedagogy of awakening	73
5 Being Nature: The Inconceivable Non-Dual Experience	99
Conclusion: A Footpath in the Woods	123
Bibliography	127
Index	129
About the Author	135

Acknowledgments

It is a pleasure to acknowledge all those who have contributed to the materialization of this book. Firstly, I thank Universidade Federal de Juiz de Fora (UFJF), Brazil, where I work in the Departamento de Ciência da Religião (Department of Religious Studies), for the continuous support. There, I would also like to thank Saulo Franco and Amanda Prado for their help with the paperwork. At Boston University, Department of English, where I wrote this book as a post-doctoral researcher, I want to thank Dr. Kevin Van Anglen and, above all, Dr. Anita Patterson for the supervision of this work, our long conversations about Thoreau and Poetry, her sharp eye, and generosity with her time. I also thank Dr. Rick Anthony Furtak and Dr. Edward F. Mooney for their careful readings, suggestions, encouragement and kind words about this work. At the Thoreau Institute and Walden Woods Project, I thank Jeff Cramer, who put the extraordinary resources of the Institute at my disposal. My thanks also to Leib Neubarth for his editing skills, to my undergraduate and graduate students for the rich discussions, and especially to the participants of the research group RENATURA (UFJF/CNPq), where all the ideas of this work were debated. I would also like to thank the Journals *Atualidade Teológica PUC-RJ* and *Caminhos PUC-GO*, for their permission to reproduce, here, two slightly different versions of chapters 4 and 5: *"Thoreau's pedagogy of awakening"* (v. 24, n. 64, pp. 87–103, jan./abr. 2020) http://www.maxwell.vrac.pucrio.br/47838/47838.PDFXXvmi=> and *"Being one with Nature: the natural non-dual experience in Thoreau"* (v. 17, n. 3, pp. 85–103, jul./dez. 2019) http://seer.pucgoias.edu.br/index.php/caminhos/article/view/7821/4298.

And with all my love, I want to thank my muse Neth and our daughter, Aída, for their patience and support.

Introduction

This book has a double root: urgency and necessity. The urgency stems from a series of crises that humankind is now facing—epidemiological, environmental, social, political, economic; however, all those crises, as many have already observed, might be better understood as different faces, or different modes, of the same underlying crisis: the Anthropocene crisis, that is, the crisis whose ultimate origins lay at our feet, triggered by the way we, humans, inhabit—and impact—this world. It seems consensual that humankind has never faced such a terrible array of combined crises that, for the first time in history, puts our very survival as a species in danger. A dense fog has alighted on this small and beautiful blue planet, and one can only hope that the pains and suffering we have been through for so long are the pangs of a childbirth—a new beginning, a new promise—, and not the gaspings of a sclerotic organism that is on the brink of its final collapse. Thence, the necessity. The necessity of a new way of inhabiting this world. And I believe that an excellent guide to teach us how to do so is Henry David Thoreau.

Living right in the middle of the Industrial Revolution and the imperial expansion of the U.S., Thoreau saw, in his own time, and in a truly prophetic way, where things were heading. Political demagoguery, the corruption of democracy, economic and spiritual slavery and natural overexploitation: sounds familiar? Those were the components of the crisis he himself witnessed first-hand and of the potential catastrophe that loomed ahead. And he did see it coming two hundred years ago. In fact, he saw it so clearly that he started writing a series of texts that, in one way or another, pointed to his utmost endeavor and hope: the need of awakening his contemporaries, blissfully asleep in religious and moral dogmas, jingoism and consumerism. As he famously states in *Walden*, he wanted to crow, like a chanticleer: "I do not propose to write an ode to dejection, but to brag as lustily as chanticleer in the morning, standing on his roost, if only to wake my neighbors up."[1]

Thus, this book is about the possibility of exploring new paths on this ancient Earth, trying to fill in new clearings in an old forest: a way of learning, or better still, relearning some things which were forgotten along the way, in fact, it is an attempt of sauntering on a trail towards awakening: a pedagogy of awakening, following in the footsteps Thoreau´s philosophical imagination. In other words, a pedagogy towards a new way of inhabiting the Earth. To try to listen, with Thoreau, to the forgotten and silenced voices of the woods, the brooks, the animals—humans or otherwise—that live outside the domesticated fences of our society and, as far as possible, to lend them our voices as well, for it seems that we have lost the ability to listen to anything but our own voices.

However, like every great pedagogue, more than advancing a set of new "truths," Thoreau seems to be much more interested in learning how to learn and the limits of learning, as when he quotes Confucius: "To know that we know what we know, and that we do not know what we do not know, that is true knowledge."[2] This new learning, though, is in fact an old one, and if one considers this new learning a pedagogy, one might, first and foremost, call it an opening, and a listening, and a looking, to the myriad voices and sights that are always and everywhere inviting us to the adventure of self-knowledge or, as I shall underline along this book, to the adventure of realizing our most profound and archaic belonging: Nature. To do so, however, implies an archeological and genealogical effort from our part. Archeological because of millennia of ideological and cultural debris that has been piling up over that most archaic experience of our true belonging, Nature. It seems we must, first and foremost, unearth the tracks before we start trailing them for, in the Western world, our Judeo-Christian, Greek and Modern European spiritual and intellectual heritages have taken pains to take us the other way around, extracting us from Her bosom. We have been taught that we are superior, supernatural beings, either because of a soul, or because of reason. This distorted outlook, I believe, lies at the origin of our most radical misunderstanding about ourselves. It was only because of our immemorial myopia that truth about ourselves could have been seen somewhere out of or above Nature.

This quest is also genealogical because, as we shall see, one of the main tenets of the referred pedagogy of awakening involves an anamnetic process to retrieve, not only our lost experience of belonging radically to Nature, but the possibility of understanding humankind as only one of the infinite modes through which Nature becomes conscious of Herself. Such lost consciousness might be read, and indeed it was, in a religious manner in the works of Thoreau. In fact, this lost connection to Nature points to the possibility of a new *religare*—a new reconnection, a new pride and joy: a new religion? As Thoreau famously said, "we ARE nature," and this new *religare* may translate his other famous dictum: "I suppose that what in other men is religion is in me love of nature."[3] Is this love of Nature, this *physiophilia*, then, to become a new religion, a new faith? Are we, at last, fated to become "faithful to the Earth," as Nietzsche exhorts the new humanity that is yet to come to be?[4] Is it possible that every single religare, from now on, will have to be, necessarily, a *renaturare*, i.e., shall our relationship with the sacred, henceforth, be mediated by a return to Nature? Is the radical green turn that every religious tradition on Earth is taking a sign that heralds a new dawn? Is our philosophical outlook and spirituality greening?

Be that as it may, it is also fair, I guess, to state at the very outset of our promenade through Thoreau's landscapes that this book is, in a certain way, the chronicle of a failure. Although I shall endeavor to present Thoreau as a philosopher-pedagogue and a poetical thinker, that is, someone whose meditations utilize not only reasoned arguments but also values the many important possibilities offered by myths, images and the whole plethora of rhetorical devices, there must be no doubt that our efforts here can only be a groping of the polyhedric and fluid membranes of his thought. Thoreau's imagination is a forest, and we must be aware that we are going to be able to saunter along and explore only some of the trails he opens for us. Indeed, this book intends to be a dialogue between Thoreau, philosophy and poetry. A poetical meditation about Thoreau's thought and poetry and the way he might help us in dwelling authentically on this world. In fact, I shall try to avoid as much as possible the plural and fertile scholarship on Thoreau, in the belief that Thoreau is the best interpreter of his own words. In this light, our main effort shall be to try to vanish, as much as possible, inside his words.

But to carry on the "root" analogy a little further, I also must say that the roots of this essay spread wide, deep and, like an Indian fig-tree (*Ficcus religiosa*), upwards also, but most importantly, backwards as well. This monograph is, in fact, a thankful recognition to Thoreau, who, among others, has been an extraordinary walking companion in my promenade through life. Written in words of light, Thoreau's works have always had the peculiar power of making me trip over epiphanies; academically, they have always fascinated me for evincing such a rich kaleidoscope of fluid borders between Philosophy, Literature, Mythology, Natural Studies, History and Religion. Such multiplicity notwithstanding, very few would deny that Nature is the center around which his thought gravitates. The mosaic of his opera—where poetry, prose, dialogue, journal, scientific essay and travelogue are clearly modes of a primal drive to expressing and actualizing his profound love of nature—is also a testimony to his creative geniality, whose unfoldings in contemporary Politics, Literature, Philosophy, Environmentalism and

Comparative Religion are some of the fields in which his original contributions are only now coming to be fully appraised. We are still in the process of discovering Thoreau. Moreover, well beyond his undeniable literary, philosophical and naturalist contributions, and echoing a venerable tradition that goes all the way back to ancient Greece, among Stoics, Epicureans and those magnificent archaic thinkers usually referred to as Presocratics, I believe that if we follow closely Thoreau's poetic meditations, we may be able to see how, according to him, a careful and tender familiarity with and the study of Nature—or living according to Nature (*physeos homologoumenos*), to underscore the epistemological/ethical nexus that translates into Stoicism's classical formula[5]—is an irreplaceable prerequisite to creating the conditions of possibility to reach that ecstatic serenity so much sought after throughout the history of Western philosophical therapeutic traditions of self-care. From this perspective, Thoreau's sapiential drive seems to be a modalization of the Western philosophical tradition that postulates the nexus between wisdom and Nature's study/contemplation, also in keeping with Spinoza's immanent or panentheistic rational soteriology's goal of "intellectual love of god or nature" (*deus sive natura*)[6], or in the ancient Greeks' concepts of "'happiness'/'serenity'" (*eudaimonia, euthymia, apatheia and ataraxia*), all of them indebted to the thesis that Nature (*physis*) is not only the origin (*arche*) of reality, but that her study and contemplation are at the genesis of a sapiential process that, ideally, could lead humans towards not only to wisdom, but to a non-dual experience that can be very well be called mystical, as we shall see further on. As Hölderlin, another lover of Greece—and Nature, puts it in his own inimitable way, describing the vertigo of that experience of non-duality with Nature:

> "To be one with all-that is the life of the divinity, that is the heaven of man. To be one with all that lives, to return in blessed self-oblivion into the All of nature, that is the summit of thoughts and joys, that is the holy mountain height, the place of eternal repose, where the midday loses its swelter and the thunder its voice and the boiling sea resembles the billowing field of grain."[7]

That, I guess, might sum up Thoreau's approach as well.

Therefore, I shall argue along the course of this stream of reflections, that the careful study of and a loving proximity to Nature, *physiophilia*, humankind included—since according to Thoreau we are part and parcel of Nature[8]—is the one true key therapeutic process, in the Greek sense[9], that opens the door both to the awakening of the highest creative potentials of human beings, as well as to the way to achieving that eudaimonic serenity. Furthermore, to pursue such a course seems promising as well, I believe, insofar as to reflect on how the study and love of Nature in Thoreau, in its many unfoldings, might contribute to exploring the possibility of reflecting about and imagine pathways where overcoming West's nihilistic legacy of metaphysics might be possible. In other words, one of the aims of this work is to inquire how Thoreau's art and thought might help us to indicate ways in which we may overcome the lack of meaning and perspectives inaugurated—according at least to a large section of Western post-modern thought—by the realization of the death of God, the collapse of metaphysics (the belief in "something beyond nature") and their attending nihilistic corollaries, maybe some of the most important of Western modernity's eventful heralds, while, at the same time, reinstating, once again, "the earth/nature" (*physis*) and faithfulness towards them.

But I anticipate myself; let me start at the very beginning, at the very root of this book. I was born and raised in Rio de Janeiro, Brazil, or, as the local Amerindian inhabitants used to call it, *Pindorama*, "the land of the Palm Trees," a place where the lace of the sea breezes softly caresses the golden meeting of the blue sky and the green canopy of the wooded mountains, enthralling all and sundry. More specifically, I was born and grew up in Tijuca, the neighborhood where Floresta da Tijuca is located—"Tijuca's Forest," the largest urban forest in the world. As a matter of fact, Floresta da Tijuca was my backyard, the building where I used to live having been built on one of its slopes, Floresta stretching upward for miles and miles of native exuberant flora and magnificent fauna.[10] It was there that I started reading—and immediately fell in love—with Thoreau. First, in an anarchist reader that included *Civil Disobedience*, then, *Walden*: I would spend the better half of a day inside Floresta, walking, reading and bathing in its superb brooks and waterfalls: sauntering, I should say. My profound admiration for Thoreau's sapiential project of living in communion with Nature impelled me to move to the mountains of Nova Friburgo, a town two and a half hours away from Rio, high up in the High Altitude Atlantic Rain Forest, where I actively participated and helped to build my first house. Not, of course, almost alone and skillfully like Thoreau, but being a clumsy help for those who seemed—only seemed—to know what they were doing. Just like Thoreau, I was exceedingly proud of my simple cottage, then. It is true, though, that it was not a perfectly built house—which I partially ascribe to substance abuse during the construction, however, it was an "authentic building," as Thoreau affirms every construction should be; besides, it was seated on a very high mountain, at the top of Cascatinha, "Little Waterfall," overlooking the town and hanging poetically from the mountain. After some time, though, with the arrival of our daughter, me and my wife had to leave it and moved into another house in the woods of Mury, Nova Friburgo, where we now live. In fact, most of this essay grew from notes that I took in my long walks on the trails that criss cross Parque Nacional dos Três Picos ("Three Peaks National

Park"), along Rio das Flores ("Flowers River") and Rio Bonito ("Beautiful River"), both of which feed Rio Macaé ("Macaé River"), which flows into the Atlantic Ocean, in an area of splendid beaches called Região dos Lagos. Thus, this book, like a mountain brook, is the sediment of many waters and crags, forests and clouds, flowers, animals and the earth; it is a strange mix of inspiration, transpiration and imagination. So, may the muses—who have lent me the words—bless it.

Albeit this work's focus on Thoreau, it is, nonetheless, a sequel to my basic philosophical interests, namely, the non-dualistic traditions of immanence, both in its Eastern avatars (Mahayana Buddhism, Advaita Vedanta and Daoism) as well as in its Western's modulations (Greek religion, Presocratics, Stoicism, Spinoza, Hölderlin); thus, this work is deeply embedded in my continued attempt to explore the philosophical possibilities of a naturalistic, immanent, non-metaphysical perspective, which I shall call along this essay, somewhat loosely, panentheistic. By panentheism, here, I mean the philosophical perspective that understands the myriad processes, phenomena and beings as an interdependent web of modes of a single Being, what the Greeks would have called *tó hólon* ("the Whole"), *tó pan* ("the All"), or, better still, in its enlarged, radical, original sense, Physis—Nature.

Thus, this book might be better understood as an attempt at a poetical reflection over the possibilities of a non-dual "Philosophy of Nature," that is, an endeavor to underscore, utilizing Thoreau's profound intuitions, the apparently forgotten fact that we *are* Nature, indeed, that we are, actually, "Nature-forgotten-of-Herself-in-us," to embrace a relatively radical non-anthropocentric perspective. Hence, my belief that many of our existential pains are corollaries of humankind's distance from Nature, the forgetfulness of our original ontological natural condition, which is masked by the many superimposed layers of cultural and social domesticating processes. Therefore, instead of proposing a "human-forgotten-of-Nature-view," I shall try to meditate on the potentially rich possibilities of understanding Philosophy—and the Sciences—as a natural, anamnetic, non-teleological process of Nature towards Self-consciousness, understanding the vascularization of consciousness in Nature, particularly in humankind, one of Nature's many epiphenomenal conscious modes, as an optimal window of opportunity for Her anamnetic process to take place. Philosophy being understood, here, therefore, as a pedagogy towards awakening from that oblivion of our natural condition. To put it simply, I believe we, this enlarged family of multifarious beings, are just masks and mirrors through which Nature manifests and explores Herself.

I will also try to advance, along the way, the thesis that Thoreau is fundamentally committed to a certain type of cognitive or philosophical endeavor that I shall call here, somewhat loosely too, *Philosophia Naturalis*, a multivalent, plural and perspectival outlook on reality, a lost art that came into existence at the very birth of Western culture, twenty-seven centuries ago on the shores of Jonia, Greece, with our wise forefathers, the archaic Greek thinkers who used to be called "Presocratics," and stretched up well into the nineteenth century, when academic specialization drew a fatal blow to that most noble and forgotten art. Thus, by *Philosophia Naturalis*, Natural Philosophy, I shall understand the interdependent, plural and holistic[11] study of Nature through the natural sciences and humanities as well, somewhat blurring the problematic borders of "hardcore" nature studies, literature and philosophy. Moreover, it is important to acknowledge the fact that Natural Philosophy pedagogy refuses to analyze a certain phenomenon in isolation and through only one perspective, mindful of the fact that to understand the part one must look at the whole, and that to understand the whole, one is supposed to understand the part, utilizing observation, imagination, scientific methodology, mythology, philosophy and poetry as well. Sadly, we seem to have irremediably lost an art that started, as far as we know, with Thales of Miletus and died away with Goethe, Alexander von Humboldt and Thoreau being two of their last adepts.

Moreover, I shall argue, as Ethel Seybold[12] and Kevin Van Anglen[13] have done more aptly before me, that Thoreau can be better understood—and savoured, through his "classicism," more specifically, his philhellenism, his love of everything Greek: myth, Philosophy, Art. Also, and most importantly, the Greeks' basic outlook on existence: realism and naturalism. Ancient Greece, that enchanted land blessed and inhabited by the Gods, was always Thoreau's ultimate criterion of truth and beauty. But maybe some clearings about what I am calling Thoreau's hellenic perspective are in order here.

Thoreau's love and admiration for everything Greek is well known. Such "Greekness," both methodologically[14] as well as to the scope of his many interests,[15] can be detected in innumerable places along his works and in a myriad of perspectives as well; right now, however, to make just a single point, that shall further on multiply in a plethora of different micro and macroscopic instances, I'd like to exemplify Thoreau's hellenic approach in his constant search for the genesis of things and phenomena: the seed, the unifying *arche* ("origin") of beings and processes, be it of an apple, a forest or Nature Herself; such a genealogical search also materializes in the quest for the original vigor, the sap, the marrow of existence, in a very particular experiencing of personal, natural and cultural phenomena. Such genealogical or genetic phenomenology, to be explored later on, may be also exemplified and subdivided in some interdependent and correlated, but autonomous fields, for a better understanding of this archaic relational grid: (i) ontologically, Thoreau's careful researches on the fundamentally paradigmatic micro-macro patterns of Nature, that infinite womb of beings and processes; in this sense, his works might very well bear the title *"Peri Physeous"* ("On Nature"), the same title attributed to most of the Presocratic works; (ii) historically/culturally, his fascination with archaic societies: Native Americans, Asiatic et al but, principally, methodologically, the Ancient Greeks; again, Herodotus' famous book title "Histories" (i.e. *historie* ["Investigations"]) comes to mind in its periegetic ambition[16] and bears testimony to Thoreau's endeavors; (iii) vitally, in terms of the correlation of world ages and individual lives, youth and early childhood are Thoreau's constant references for the "perfect state," here resembling Wordsworth and Hölderlin: i.e., Greece as the "childhood" of humankind; (iv) calendar wise, Springtime, the point of departure of the natural cycles, the radicle of Nature Herself takes pride of place; (v) as a part of the day, morning or, better still, dawn, the "auroreal," heroic moment of supreme freshness; (vi) linguistically, we can subdivide his genealogical approach further: (a) semantically, etymology furnishes the best tool, due to his belief that, originally, words signify things, the more into the archaic structure of words and languages one goes, the nearer one gets to its pristine, original semantic absolute value, Thoreau being particularly fit to such a task due to his linguistic skills and training in both old and modern languages; (b) in terms of language register, poetry, or more precisely, the mythopoetical discourse, since it is the one closest to the source, is the linguistic register that best captures Being's multifarious original richness. Thoreau's well known love of Homer, Greek mythology, and his translations of Aeschylus attest to his saying that only in Greek mythology Nature speaks for Herself, as we shall see further on. Thus, when he sings his love of Nature, archaic societies, youth, Spring, myth, poetry, he is, I believe, fundamentally singing an eulogy to different modes of the basic phenomenon: proximity to the Source, for, as he himself points out: "we want most to dwell near to . . . the perennial source of our life,"[17] the "source" in question offering many possible avenues of interpretation, but apparently alluding to the rationale behind this genealogical look and the correspondence between those instantiations ("Greece-Spring-youth-dawn"), providing us not only with a grid of correlative micro-meso-macro phenomena but also with a powerful methodological and pedagogical tool to better capture Thoreau's overarching attachment to primeval and archaic dynamics in many different areas of interest as well. Pursuing each one of those avenues backwards, both in terms of an archaic, primeval level of experience before the fossilization of History, Culture and Society, but inwards as well, in terms of proximity and intimacy to the more "embryonic" experiential levels of reality, that genealogical effort would, ultimately, place us in the "existential knot" that represents both an experience of disalienation in terms of a personal quasi-soteriological, libertarian experience, but to a better understanding of the continuing "fall" that plagues humankind's history from a more radical and positive relationship with

Nature before the progressive, and in a certain sense necessary, artificialization and falsification that socio-cultural domestication imposes on us.

All those powerful images (Greece-youth-Spring-dawn) being different symbols of the same arcane reality to be detected either, microscopically, within ourselves or, externally, macroscopically, in Nature and History. To sum up: I believe Thoreau is Greek. There is a delightful and illustrative story that Thoreau tells us about his "Greek-holistic" approach that may help us to clarify this point:

> The secretary of the Association for the Advancement of Science requests me, as he probably has thousands of others, by a printed circular letter from Washington the other day, to fill the blank against certain questions, among which the most important one was what branch of science I was especially interested in, using the term science in the most comprehensible sense possible. Now, though I could state to a select few that department of human inquiry which engages me, and should be rejoiced at an opportunity to do so, I felt that it would be to make myself the laughing-stock of the scientific community to describe or attempt to describe to them the branch of specially interests me, inasmuch as they do not believe in a science which deals with the higher law. So I was obliged to speak to their condition and describe to them that poor part of me which alone they can understand. The fact is I am a mystic, a trancedentalist, and a natural philosopher to boot. Now I think of it, I should have told them at once that I was a transcendentalist. That would have been the shortest way of telling them that they would not understand my explanations.

Most commentators have, in a very fecund way, dedicated a lot of attention to this passage trying to explore Thoreau's multiple interests and his incapacity to pinpoint exactly where his main field of interest lies. Such incapacity has reverberated in Thoreau's scholarship in terms of what exactly he was trying to do or be ("writer, mystic, naturalist, philosopher"). However, I believe that the sequence of this passage has been relatively neglected, and it offers a key not only to a better understanding of the extract, but it also sheds light on Thoreau's main methodological and philosophical affiliation:

> "How absurd that, though I probably stand as near to nature as any of them and am by constitution as good an observer as most, yet a true account of my relation to nature should excite their ridicule only! If it had been the secretary of an association of which Plato and Aristotle was the president, I should not have hesitated to describe my studies at once and particularly."[18]

Thoreau's relation with Nature was plural, idiosyncratic and revolutionary. Plural because it consisted of many different perspectives. As we shall see later, an empiricist methodology, that is, observing and cataloguing the results in a quantitative way, would simply not do. Idiosyncratic because it was, among many tenets, a mix of trained observation, philosophical musing, poetical meditation and delicate fascination. Moreover, Nature's observation was never an end in itself: it served higher purposes. That is why he fears scientists would ridicule him. I believe it is very instructive that Thoreau singles out two Greek thinkers, Plato and Aristotle, whose plural interests unfolded into a herculean attempt to investigate many branches of knowledge having a final global, holistic, sapiential perspective at the basis of their endeavor: what Greeks used to call "Philosophy," "love of wisdom" or, in Thoreau's terms, "sympathy with intelligence." Such sympathy may well be called an openness towards every bit of knowledge that, once arranged in a symphonic intuition, might be conducive to a state of serenity, aesthetical and ecstatic contemplation. His method was indeed a "Method" in a teleological and one might even say "quasi-soteriological" way: something which one takes to a certain end or finality. The end, the finality of his method, as I shall try to present it, points to an experience, a radical experience of non-duality with Nature. An awareness, as I said earlier on, not only that we are Nature, but also that we are Nature experiencing Herself through us. This inconceivable, or one might say, mystical experience, is not the fruit of any specific religious ascesis—albeit some of its components do seem to partake of asceticism—or Thoreau's asceticism at any rate. More than asceticism, however, that experience is, I believe, the optimal result of a profound and tender nearness to Nature. Inhabiting it not as a visitor, but as a conscious part and parcel of it. That is why I am calling his approach to Nature a "pedagogy," a willingness to relearn, reopen, reconnect: it is in fact a return and not an advancement or accumulation of new knowledge. Thus, one might call the whole process not only a pedagogy, but a *paideia* as well, the word in question being the one the Greeks used to point to their educational process as a continuum of music, physical activity, literature, practical knowledge and the pursuit of wisdom. And returning to his above quotation—by now certainly forgotten, it is certainly not by chance that he picks two of classical Greece´s most influential thinkers to point to his true philia, his ultimate intellectual belonging and affiliation. As he pointedly says somewhere else: "Philosophy is a Greek word by good rights, and it stands almost for a Greek thing."[19] More than just advancing a substantive defense of Philosophy in its Greek, radical sense, Thoreau seems to be not only championing a very particular affiliation to a certain tradition of producing and reproducing knowledge, but also hinting at something deeper here, the very meaning of Philosophy itself. Elsewhere, he deepens his look: "we have all of us by nature *mánteumáte* (as both Plato and Aristotle call it), a certain divination, presage and parturient vaticination in our minds, of some higher good and perfection than either power or knowledge." Aristotle himself declares, that there *is lógou ti kreîtton*, which is *lógou arkhé*,—(something better than reason and knowledge, which is the principle and original of all).[20]

It is interesting to note how, throughout Thoreau's works, in a very Greek philosophical way, he seems to search not only the sense, the meaning, an answer; rather, he seems to be endeavoring to search the perpetual condition of searching, searching the "arche," the very genesis of the condition of searching, the quest itself. If what Aristotle says is true, if the principal condition to philosophize is, fundamentally, wonder,[21] Thoreau certainly subscribes to it. It is the search that materializes as sense, as meaning, since the result—ultimately corrupted as "truth"—is always open-ended in its possibility. "Sense," "meaning," "the answer," the "truth" is always a variable, subjective, provisional affair, unlike the search, the quest. This seems to be one of the possible avenues for understanding his definition of Philosophy as "sympathy with intelligence." This sympathy, this *philia*, to use the Greek word, generally translated as "love," Philosophy being traditionally understood and translated as "love of wisdom," seems to point to the old Greek conception of Philosophy as a perpetual search, as an open-ended quest, much more a method, a way of living, than a set of sclerotic systematic truths or, as he says in unmistakably mournful tones: "There are nowadays professors of philosophy, but not philosophers."[22] In one of his most important philosophical statements, and pregnant of beauty, he puts it:

> "My desire for knowledge is intermittent; but my desire to bathe my head in atmospheres unknown to my feet is perennial and constant. The highest state that we can attain to is not Knowledge, but Sympathy with intelligence. I do not know that this higher knowledge amounts to anything more definite than a novel and grand surprise on a sudden revelation of the insufficiency of all we called Knowledge before—a discovery that there are more things in heaven and earth than are dreamed of in our philosophy."[23]

When one inquires, when one poses questions about what one does not know, one is putting into practice the true philosophical and scientific dimension of the search, as Thoreau says in a very peculiar Aristotelian tone: "I do not know that knowledge amounts to anything more definite than a novel and grand surprise, or a sudden revelation of the insufficiency of all that we had called knowledge before; an indefinite sense of the grandeur and glory of the universe."[24] Moreover, in a truly Socratic way: "It is only when we forget all our learning that we begin to know."[25] And again, as ironically as Socrates:

> "I have heard that there is a Society for the Diffusion of Useful Knowledge. It is said that knowledge is power and the like. Methinks there is equal need of a

Society for the Diffusion of Useful Ignorance, for what is most of our boasted so-called knowledge but a conceit that we know something, which robs us of the advantages of our actual ignorance."[26]

Such a mode of being-in-the-search-of, this utmost scientific and philosophical openness, is the condition towards which Thoreau seems to invite us to reach and implement. In this sense, the answers—any answers—are just necessary unfolding of that openness, of that mode of inquiry; in other words, it is Science and Philosophy manifesting themselves with provisional and rectifiable answers. This methodology, this philosophical way of life, the very radical condition of the questioning subject, seems to be embraced by Thoreau in his quest for the perpetual condition of the questing itself, the intellectual "heroic" dimension of self- and Nature's knowledge; answers, be they what they may, are only corollaries, epiphenomena of that searching, of the inquiry, of the questioning itself. That intellectual "heroic" way of life discloses Thoreau's debt to the Greek concept of "historia," the "inquiry," the "open investigation" of phenomena, and this very openness antagonizes him with every kind of dogmatism—though he himself sometimes indulges in them—that he rebels against. His visceral dislike of any dogmas whatsoever, his relentless and sharp criticism of his contemporaries' beliefs, the inherited dogmas, the sclerotic social "truths" he barely manages to conceal his despising of, the "cattlelicism" of his fellow Concordians, all these assume vital importance in his carefully crafted critique of inherited experience as well. In this perspective, one should remember that that line of investigation, or, better still, that methodological approach to phenomena, overarches the whole of Thoreau's writings: from *Natural History of Massachusetts* until his last published essays, both in life and posthumously, all subscribe to that Greek holistic approach, later on to be sacrificed on the altar of academic specialization. To sum up Thoreau's project—and Western's wisdom and scientific knowledge program in a nutshell, by the way—I cannot think of anything better than Emerson's prophetic exhortation contained in his *American Scholar*: "and, in fine, the ancient precept 'Know thyself,' and the modern precept 'Study nature,' become at last one maxim."[27] Self-knowledge and Nature study, as I hope to be able to point out along this text, encapsulate precisely Thoreau's basic drive, maybe unconsciously rising to Emerson's challenge and incorporating the very Natural Philosophy project itself, the hallmark of Western's intellectual trajectory, together with the Delphic invitation to self-scrutiny, another characteristic of our sapiential tradition. Thoreau, I truly believe, has a lot to teach us in both dimensions.

Moreover, I also intend to inquire into the possibility of thinking that already referred to anamnetic philosophical process as a "Pedagogy of awakening," to underline Henry's fascination with the "dawn," the auroreal awakening, the experiential potentiality that lies hidden inside all of us, whose external correlate becomes a figurative comparison and constant point of reference throughout his writings for the inner overcoming of our sleeping condition. From the set of homiletic denunciations of his alienated sleeping contemporaries he wishes to awaken like a Chanticleer, to the symptomatology he draws at the beginning of *Walden*, it is important to try to detect the possible practices that may conduce to the eudaimonic state that ensues from the adoption of the said therapy. Such a Pedagogy, dispersed as it is through his writings, is worthwhile to trying to retrieve it in its integrity, since the reward, that eudaimonic experience which I shall characterize as a non-dual experience of merging with Nature, seems to be the goal towards which Thoreau strives to achieve in his intimacy with the natural world.

However, again, more than an "ecstasy" or "instasy," I believe that experience could be better understood as *"aesthesis,"* an aesthetical, sensual, elemental fruition of the necessary interdependence between subject and object, humankind and Nature, a Nature to which we intrinsically belong, which envelops and surrounds us, a Nature that, its centrality in his thought notwithstanding, is rarely systematically articulated in terms of a general and exhaustive theory of Nature, what one could technically call a "Philosophy of Nature." More like a pointillist picture, whose general effect is the result of a plethora of minimal views—which I shall call an epistemological perspectivism or epistemological sauntering when "in praxis," along this essay—Thoreau's recurrent effort to observe a fact from a plurality of perspectives not only enhances our horizon of research as well as deepens the richness of details that contours each phenomenon he describes against the backdrop of our clumsy and blurring lack of attention.

Another of my interests in pursuing this research is the possibility of inquiring over the potential of what I shall call "wild thought" and the characterization of Thoreau as a "wild" thinker. By "wild" I understand the non-domesticated, non-sedentary thought, a nomadic approach, an epistemological sauntering, a view from diverse perspectives and in different moments, each one helping to paint that pointillist picture referred to above, which one might as well call "perspectivism."

Such "wild" perspective, I believe, is a handy tool to explore Thoreau's "ecology of immanence," the understanding of the continuum between humans and Nature, which may be contrasted to the "sociology of difference," the dichotomic approach that splits humans and Nature. In this light, I will explore two correlate phenomena that, I guess, are at the very base of our domesticated, sclerotic civilization: architecture-building and agriculture-planting, as examples of that domesticating process. Thoreau, as we shall see, has a lot to say about both processes, since he was a both a builder as well as a tiller whose emphasis on sustainable, sacramental agriculture and building are radical and innovative contributions to Western thought. But to introduce synthetically the two questions, which I will elaborate later on: what do architecture and agriculture mean and what do they have in common?

Both, I shall argue, are techniques; both are correlate phenomena in the process of humankind's sedentation. First, I would like to explore the tension between architecture and Nature, stressing architecture's carving out of Nature a *domus*, a "seat," a "house." However, as we know, from domus comes dominion, first the *de facto*, and then the juridical appropriation of what is common into private, particular usage and exploitation: the obverse of dominion, though, is domestication, another word that comes from domus, the civilizational seed that expels us from the intimacy with Nature and brings about the necessary sclerosis of the nomadic drive. As I shall discuss further on, according to Thoreau, a large part of our alienation from Nature can be ascribed to the successive layers of techniques and instruments that society superimposes onto the natural world. Another such technique is agriculture, "the cultivation of the ager," the domestication and instrumentalization of the fields, of the wilderness; again, such domestication implies a violence, a dominion, a segmentation and ulterior appropriation of wilderness and her fruits, that ultimately becomes, for Thoreau, a burden from which his hapless Concordian contemporaries could not manage to escape from. Those two techniques are exemplary to illustrate the interdependent process of the dominion of Nature and its necessary corollary, our voluntary subjugation to the socio-political-juridical and economical structures that morph into extremely problematic ethical and philosophical implications, debasing and corrupting our natural, most originary affiliation.

Another characteristic of this essay is an engagement with Thoreau's poetry. Thoreau's poetry has been, I am afraid, sadly neglected. More than advancing an aesthetical evaluation of his poems, or contributing to the history of literary studies, I want to emphasize his poetical production as a privileged source to understanding some of his most important experiences, poetry being, in his personal scale of communication tools, second only to music, of which we shall talk a lot as well.

Finally, some words about the division of this monograph. This work is divided in five parts or chapters. The first one, "Concord, Cosmos" is an introduction to some methodological considerations and concepts that will illuminate this work: Nature, familiarity with it, roots and a plethora of related terms that will, further on, help in reflecting upon the possibilities of inhabiting the Earth in a more enlightened way.

The second chapter, "The long shadow of Prometheus: civilization and alienation," shall tackle the many problems involved in our assertion that our alienated ontological condition is directly related to a set of socio-cultural mechanisms that help to hide our "naturalness." Such alienation is carefully analyzed by Thoreau in the opening pages of Walden, his chiaroscuro masterpiece, where almost every chapter contrast with the previous one, so that the contours of things and phenomena get more vivid and sharp. The result of that analysis is an important propedeutic step towards the organization of the remainder of our essay.

We then proceed to the third chapter: "Sacramental Technique," to try to figure out some very important concepts in Thoreau's conceptual lace: his understanding of Nature and Her relationship to Culture, necessarily highlighting the many tensions and inconclusive theses that come up in such dimension if one bears in mind Thoreau's refusal to develop and elaborate a systematic definition of such terms.

Our fourth stop, "Being wild: Thoreau's Pedagogy of awakening," will endeavor to amplify the possibilities of imagining Thoreau's writings as providing a sort of "savage" Pedagogy, a set of intuitions and practices, political and economic included, that seem to stem from his continuous pointing to the need for a more profound relationship with Nature. Such intimacy with the natural world presupposes not only nearness—one may be near something or someone and not be intimate—but effective and deliberate careful engagement. To think his strategies of careful proximity as a "Pedagogy" shall prove, I believe, extremely tempting, more so if one compares it with Ancient Greece's philosophical traditions of self-care which took the study of Nature as their fundamental theses towards a fulfilling and serene life.

Finally, we turn to the possible results of the said Pedagogy, an experience of non-duality between humans and Nature: "Being Nature, the inconceivable non-dual experience"; there we shall try to assemble from many disconnected fragments of Thoreau's writings a set of testimonials that seem to point to a quasi-soteriological experience, where language shows its limits in conveying the vertigo and inconceivability of such a metanoic non-dualistic experience.

NOTES

1. Thoreau, H. D. *Walden*, Princeton: Princeton University Press, 1971, p. 84. (Henceforth *Walden*).
2. *Walden*, p. 11.
3. Thoreau, H. D. *Journal: Volume 2*. Edited by Robert Sattelmeyer. Princeton: Princeton University Press, 1984. (Pj.2.55).
4. Niezsche, F. *The Portable Nietzsche*. New York: Viking, 1982, p. 125.
5. Diogenes Laertius. *Lives Of Eminent Philosophers*, vol. Ii. Loeb Classical Library. Cambridge: Harvard University Press, 1995, p. 195.
6. Spinoza. *Spinoza's Complete Works*. Indianapolis: Hackett, p. 321.

7. Hölderlin, F. *Hyperion, Or The Hermit In Greece*. Translated by Ross Benjamin, New York: Archipelago, 2008.

8. Thoreau, H. D. *Collected Essays And Poems*. The Library Of America, Vol. 124. New York : The Library Of America, 2001 (Henceforth: Name Of The Poem/Essay *Cep*, Page Number). Walking, *Cep* p. 225.

9. In The Sense Of Recovering Our "Healthy Perspective" Towards Nature.

10. In Fact Floresta Da Tijuca Is Partially Native—On Its Highest Gradients—And Partially Replanted With Native Species By Major Archer And Seven Unnamed Slaves On Old Coffee Plantations Of Tijuca's Plateau, Under The Auspices Brazil's Last Emperor, Dom Pedro Ii, During The Second Half Of The Nineteenth Century To Safeguard Some Of Rio's Water Sources. Unfortunately, Today, *Floresta* Is Suffering From The Inordinate Spread Of The City, Encroaching Upon It Like A Relentless And Merciless Predator.

11. Although I Don't Like The Expression *Holistic* Due To Some Unfortunate Contemporary New Age Misusages And Misunderstandings Of The Term, It Is Precisely What Such An Endeavor Should Be Named, Faithful To The Greek Expression—And Objective, *Tó Hólon*, The "Whole."

12. Seybold, E. *Thoreau: The Quest And The Classics*. New Haven: Yale University Press, 1951.

13. Van Anglen K. P. And Engell, J. (Editors) *The Writings Of Thoreau: Translations. Princeton University Press, Princeton, 1986*, Introduction. *Thoreau's Epic Ambitions: A Walk To Wachusett And The Persistence Of The Classics In An Age Of Science* In *The Call Of Classical Literature In The Romantic Age*, Edited and with an Introduction by K. P. Van Anglen And James Engell, Edimburgh: Edinburgh University Press, 2017.

14. In Terms Of Methodology, His Attempt To An Overarching, Unifying Principle, A *Unity* That Underlies The Myriad Phenomena, Detected And Construed On His *Perspectivism*, As I Shall Have The Opportunity To Expand Later On, All Of His Perspectives Wrapped Up In Mythopoetic Language.

15. Philosophy, Art, Politics, Ethnology And So Many Others.

16. Herodotus Periegetic Mix Of History, Geography, Ethography, *Curio* And Travelogue Bring To Mind *A Week On The Concord And Merrimack Rivers, The Maine Woods, Cape Cod Et Al.*

17. *Walden*, p. 133.

18. Thoreau, H. D. *The Journal Of H. D. Thoreau In Fourteen Volumes Bound As Two*. New York: Dover, 1962 (Henceforth *Journal*, Unless Specified). *Journal*, vol. V, p. 529, My Italics.

19. *Journal*, vol. Xiii, p. 29.

20. *Journal*, vol. Ii, p. 150. We Shall Have A Lot More To Say About That As We Proceed.

21. Aristotle. *The Basic Works Of Aristotle*. New York: Modern Library, 2001. *Metaphysics* A, 982b, p. 692.

22. *Walden*, p. 14.

23. *Walking, Cep*, p. 250.

24. *Journal*, vol. Ii, p. 168.

25. *Journal*, vol. Xii, p. 371.
26. *Journal*, vol. Ii, p. 150.
27. Emerson, R. W. *Essays And Letters*. New York: The Library Of America, 1983. *The American Scholar*, p. 56.

Chapter 1

Concord, Cosmos

CONCORD

Henry David Thoreau did many things, was many things and, because of that, represent distinct things for different people: writer, teacher, philosopher, naturalist, poet, translator, environmentalist, builder, political agitator, musician, saunterer, mystic, surveyor, anarchist, pencil manufacturer, traveller, tiller and enlightened vagabond. However, those are only some of his many occupations. Here, along this trail that we now begin, through the dense foliage of his imagination's landscapes, I will try to underline Thoreau, the thinker and pedagogue. More than any of his "occupations," Thoreau reflected in a sustained way, with care and originality, about teaching, writing, building, tilling and his other occupations as well. Here is the thinker: someone who thinks his life and lives his thought in its singularity, grandeur, weakness and limits. In this perspective, Thoreau was a true philosopher, someone who incorporated reflection into the very fabric of his existence. Indeed, Thoreau lived a life of action, thinking and meditation, and bequeathed us a testimony of what was most genuine in him, following the very same rule that he set for himself and everyone else, either in life or art: sincerity.[1] To be sincere, to be authentic, that is, to be and accept what one is, this great 'yes saying' to oneself—and inasmuch as possible to the world, since sometimes he was at war with it—in Thoreau translates the outcome of a perennial self-scrutiny, a profound and tender engagement with both himself and Nature. Such a constant engagement with himself and Nature, though, and his relative physical distance from society took its toll: a perceived aloofness and coldness of heart. The vast majority of testimonies, made by some very acute and astute observers, does not leave much room for doubt. Thoreau lived only half-heartedly with society and his fellow humans. With *society and his fellow humans*. It is important to make this point, because as poor as his philanthropy was,[2] ultimately, all his literary, philosophical and pedagogical efforts had his fellow Concordians in sight, and when I italicize "society" and "fellow humans," one has to remember how his heart went out for wild nature, its inhabitants and, obliquely, to his fellow citizens.

As we embark on the adventure of engaging with Thoreau's thought, it is necessary, I believe, in a propedeutic manner, to get acquainted with the world he inhabited, the Nature he loved and the books he cherished, since they all spill over into his work. It is important to develop an intimacy, a nearness to him, so that we can better approach his views. We must befriend him to be allowed to penetrate inside the inner workings of his brilliant mind. Intimacy, here, means much more than proximity, for beings may be near each other and do not be intimate at all. The intimacy alluded to here is a caring, a loving and tender openness towards the other. A willingness to engage affectionately with everyone and everything that flourishes in our personal horizon, to be able to sympathize and listen to their voices. In Thoreau's words: "the finest qualities of our nature, like the bloom on fruits, can be preserved only by the most delicate handling. Yet we do not treat ourselves nor one another thus tenderly."[3] Otherwise, how is one supposed to understand someone or something without being near to it, with care and patience? Lack of an attentive care breeds distance; distance, estrangement; estrangement, forgetfulness; hence the need of an anamnetic endeavour to retrieve our lost affective connections, the necessity of a delicate touch on the skin of reality, so that reality might open itself up to us.

Thus, it seems fitting, now, to remember Thoreau's circumstantiality in order to know him better and, ideally, to be capable of understanding his habitat, and appreciate how and why he did what he did and thought what he thought, so that we can, together, also rethink the way we inhabit this world or, ideally, as he puts it, how we can be able to "elevate our lives by a conscious endeavour."[4] Like every great thinker, Thoreau helps us not only to understand more things or more profoundly those things but, first and foremost, he helps us precisely in how to approach things, so that the result of such an approaching may translate either in specific knowledge, contemplation or celebration.

"What do we want most to dwell near to? . . . the perennial source of our life."[5] There can be no doubt that, for Thoreau, his small and valiant village of Concord, where he was born and raised, with its streets, houses, people, woods, its beasts, brooks, trees and flowers, was the true source of his life, his habitat and horizon, his ground and home: the perennial source from where he watched society and nature, and from where he extracted the ambrosia of his thought and poetry. There, he found everything he needed in terms of objects—and subjects—for observation and reflection: the village, the surrounding woods, the ponds. Economy, ecology: Concord was his *oikos*, his home, and it was there he found his *"oikeiosis,"*⁶ his belonging, his familiarity, be it with people and beasts, buildings and woods, streets and ponds. It was from this local scenario that his work was able to achieve the impressive universality of reach we witness today. Being truly local, he became universal, since the universality of the experience, certainly, has nothing to do with "Concord" itself, but with every "Concord" where people experience their belonging as radically as he experienced his. Deeply rooted in his habitat, Thoreau was a singular flowering of his native environment as much as his fellow Concordians, the muskrats and fishes that inhabited, with him, those places. The symphonic music played by the myriad voices that he could hear when he tuned to that self-opening experience of being deeply ingrained in his most archaic belonging, his natural circumstantiality, was rewarded by moving experiences of non-duality, or a deep integration with nature. As to society, his sharp criticisms notwithstanding, one can feel a profound concern for his fellow citizens as well: trouble is, albeit Thoreau saw no great distinction between Nature and Culture, there can be no doubt he was unwaveringly partial to the first one.

Concord, and its surroundings, provided him with everything he needed in terms of objects of study and subjects for reflection: the village, Politics, Economy, Social mores; the woods: Botany, Ethology and others. Thus, his native place and its surroundings offered him a palette of rich colours with which he was able to paint his pointillistic masterpieces, reflecting the extraordinary richness he was capable of perceiving in such a comparatively small universe. The radicality of his meditations and writings belongs intrinsically to Concord, Walden, and all the places he was able to morph with: he became a self-conscious Concord, and a self-conscious Walden: through him, Concord and Walden became conscious of themselves. If we believe in Emerson's testimony, Thoreau had the ability of becoming as immobile as a rock or a piece of wood for long periods, becoming just another piece of the landscape, so much so that birds pecked his hair and snakes gathered at his feet.⁷ That is not surprising, for doesn't he himself ask: "Shall I not have intelligence with the earth? Am I not partially leaves and vegetable mould myself?"⁸

This intelligence, the communication and dialogue with earth, the woods and its inhabitants, mirrors the recognition of our affiliation with the elemental constitution of our dwelling landscape and amplifies the horizon of our inquiry, pointing, unequivocally, to Thoreau's deeply ingrained sense of interdependence with his natural surroundings. This morphing capacity, this quiet, attentive and tender ability of blending with his environment speaks volumes about his method of relating to reality, which echoes in the way he inhabited that world, and created the conditions of possibility for him to fulfil in an innovative and singular way his artistic, philosophical and scientific mission. Thoreau was a mosaic, not because he was particularly composed of many strata and dimensions—most beings are—but because he was able to open himself up in such a tender and radical manner towards the other, natural or otherwise, that he became what he was dedicating his attention to. So plastic was his constitution that, when his brother John died of lockjaw in his arms, Thoreau manifested the symptoms of the disease himself for some time after the event. By examining and auscultating, that is, listening with attention and care, the mores of his distant, but beloved Concord fellow citizens, and singing its woods, fauna and flora, he created a tableau of images, sounds and feelings that refuse a partition between Culture and Nature: "I did not see why I might not make a book on Cape Cod, as well as my neighbor on 'Human Culture.' It is but another name for the same thing."[9] Walden, Cape Cod, Concord: that gapless continuum between Nature and Culture is extraordinarily important and I shall explore it further on, since that is the core around which he framed the conditions to achieving that serenity and singularity that stemmed from an authentic, radical, non-dual perception that he himself was a conscious and indivisible filament of the totality of beings, processes and phenomena: Nature. Overcoming the opposition Nature x Culture by developing an appositional perspective between them, Thoreau experienced with aesthetical and ecstatic awe the magnificence and munificence of Nature, so much so that he was able—competent surveyor he was—to draw a careful map, a precise topography of the trail towards awakening to that non-dual dimension: a topology of ecstatic beauty and wisdom.

It was there, in Concord, on the 12th of July of 1817, that Henry David Thoreau was born.[10] It was there that he breathed his last on May 6th, 1862. Except for his sojourn at Harvard, a brief stint in New York, a few trips around New England, and a couple of other brief journeys to Canada and Minnesota, Thoreau's life was remarkably local, gravitating around Concord like a satellite around a planet whose gravity pull is too strong to be broken. There, his life flowed smoothly, like the waters of his beloved Concord river, whose eulogy he sang in his first book, *A week on the Concord and Merrimack rivers*. It was there, in Concord, that he was born and raised; more important, it was there that he decided to inhabit. It was there that the elements that made up his constitution morphed with his surroundings. His mimicry with his native place was so profound that it became impossible to separate him from a tree branch, lichen on a rock, a bend of a crystal-clear brook or a street of the village. He lived in them, and through him they became conscious of themselves. His artistry may be understood, in this light, as a lending of voices to those mute beings that inhabited his world, and towards whom he developed an extraordinary sympathy, literally, "the capacity of being affected with." This affection was displayed in caring attention, and if Thoreau was able to speak in such a remarkable manner, not about Nature, but *for* Nature and *as* Nature, we my rest assured that the sympathy was mutual, rocks and trees lending him their silent presence as mirrors where he could see himself reflected, and windows through which he saw the whole. As we shall see, that mimicry was so pervasive that he sang his being as Walden Pond or, better still, Walden Pond found in Thoreau the best possible mouthpiece, an unsurpassed creative medium through whom it could and would sing its interdependent song with Thoreau. The convergence was mutual: the breezes, the waters, the grass, the birds, his hut: all those beings spoke of secrets they all shared together, and he was capable, medium of Nature as he was, to paint them in such a masterly way. The interstices between himself and Nature were over. The luminous hiatus that served to clear cut himself from the woods and its dwellers had been long erased. That, as I hope to be able to depict, was not a deliberate program but, fundamentally, a conscious effort of his part that consisted in a novel way of relating to phenomena. It was, plain and simple, Thoreau being himself, that is, just the continuous experience of remembering his most archaic condition, that of a natural being. His singularity, his unique ability, was to be able to become like a flute, like the one he himself used to play, on the lips of Nature. She played, through him, Her infinite songs. She became conscious of Herself through him. He was so deeply ingrained within "The Maiden," as he affectionately calls Her, that the ominous gap we have created between ourselves and Nature was bridged, by him, with a rainbow of truth and beauty. More impressively, he circulated in the woods with the same familiarity that he used to frequent the pages of Homer, Aeschylus and some of his other life-long classical companions. This is very important because it was there, in the treasure of ancient Greek myth that he found inspiration and dialogue with Nature in its printed voice. Therefore, his source was not only Concord or Walden. It was Homer's Ilion, Aeschylus' Thebes—their Concords, his Ilion and Thebes. That radicular belonging to a place, to be so deeply ingrained in a certain landscape, allowed him to participate in every authentic dwelling, to attend the multiple landscapes in which others lived and portrayed as authentically as he did, be it the pages of the Iliad, or a swamp in an outback. That is why I believe that when he states that he wants "to dwell near the perennial source of [his] life," the "source" in question was not only a natural, physical one, rather, it meant dwelling in a radical experience of living attuned to that most archaic experience of inhabiting, of belonging together, of "*oikeiosis*"—to be able to be conscious of partaking a common *oikos*—, a common home, with everything that flourishes with us, this infinite concert of myriad voices, what he calls his "Aeolian harp"; in other words, to be able to awaken, to experience and sing the glorious dawn of beauty and truth, to live in a perennial child-like condition of openness towards novelty, to live in the

Springtime of our hearts, in sum, to be Greek. In his eulogy of the ancients we hear:

> "The student may read Homer or Æschylus in the Greek without danger of dissipation or luxuriousness, for it implies that he in some measure emulate their heroes, and consecrate morning hours to their pages. The heroic books, even if printed in the character of our mother tongue, will always be in a language dead to degenerate times; and we must laboriously seek the meaning of each word and line, conjecturing a larger sense than common use permits out of what wisdom and valor and generosity we have . . . For what are the classics but the noblest recorded thoughts of man? They are the only oracles which are not decayed, and there are such answers to the most modern inquiry in them as Delphi and Dodona never gave. We might as well omit to study Nature because she is old . . . Homer has never yet been printed in English, nor Æschylus, nor Virgil even,—works as refined, as solidly done, and as beautiful almost as the morning itself; for later writers, say what we will of their genius, have rarely, if ever, equalled the elaborate beauty and finish and the life long and heroic literary labors of the ancients."[11]

This recurring set of images: hero, heroic, morning, summer, Greece, myth, Nature, beauty, genius, truth, is telling, and we shall return to them repeatedly, yet, for Thoreau, those ancients' heroic, auroreal language is a dead one for those who cannot dwell in that experience of radically belonging to a place. For those, though, who can really experience the radicality of dwelling in their habitat, that is, to live sincerely and authentically within their surroundings—be it landscapes or books—, they all share a common language, a language that is spoken through a different medium, creating a fraternity of dwellers that are able to communicate throughout time. Thoreau lives with Homer and Aeschylus perpetually in that dimension of truth and beauty because they lived authentically and sincerely, thus creating a lingo that was universal and atemporal. We shall have ample opportunity of returning to that grid, where Thoreau connects those points into a polyhedric sculpture of meanings. He did inhabit Concord, Walden, Troy, Thebes, and frequented Homer and Aeschylus and Virgil because they all spoke the very same language: the language of belonging—the language of authenticity and sincerity.

That is the rationale why this poetical meditation on inhabiting Concord—his Cosmos—is decisive for our efforts here for a number of reasons, and the history of the word "habitat," the place one inhabits, may help us to better understand its many unfoldings. The noun "habitat" and its verbal form, to inhabit, come from the intensive form of the Latin verb "habere," "to own," "to possess"; Hence, to inhabit means to possess a place, but more than owning a certain tract of land or a building, it appears to point towards having one's nature deeply rooted in a certain surrounding, in a certain set of circumstances that, on one hand determine our nature and, on the other hand, is determined by our inhabiting within it. Our surroundings determine us as much as we ourselves determine our surrounding landscapes, by the way we live, act and impact the place. The landscape transforms us as much as we transform the landscape. This dialogical tension with our environment—it is indeed a dialogue of sorts, precludes, as I said, the ownership for, as he beautifully puts it in his creative reconstruction of the excursion he and his brother did on the Concord and Merrimack rivers, he truly inhabited, he truly belonged there because he did not own the landscape: "how fortunate were we who did not own an acre of those shores, who had not renounced our title to the Whole. One who knew how to appropriate the true value of this world would be the poorest man in it. The poor rich man! All he has is what he has bought."[12]

The true value of this world, to inhabit it consciously as one of its flowerings in the symphony of the Whole, translates the belonging to the landscape, to be able to distill from it the primeval experience of being what oneself already is—Nature. This, of course, demands the ability of being capable of listening attentively to and leaning in the direction of a calling, a calling from the wilderness. As we lean towards the wilderness, the wilderness seems to lean towards us, opening herself up to us and making us engage in a dialogue of self-discovery and appreciation with her. This convergence between us and Nature, between us and our most archaic identity, is the basic condition of possibility towards the referred pedagogy of awakening. A pedagogy that starts in contemplation, is transformed within us in meditation, to finally reach the sphere of action. That "sacramental" relationship precludes, as mentioned, the ownership for, according to Henry, to possess the landscape in the juridical meaning, impoverishes us, in as much as what we possess, in the economic sense, finally ends up possessing us; as we shall see further on, we become "tools of our tools" and, in the process, by possessing a fragment, one has to let go of the Whole.

Thus, the Thoureauvian way of dwelling seems to mean, to use one of his favourite hieroglyphs, a "sacramental" manner of inhabiting a landscape as a singular rooting of ourselves in our most original soil, Nature, deeply spiking our feet in earth so that our arms, like the canopy of a tree, can extend in thankful reverence and exuberance towards the sky. The continuum of man, sky, earth, the woods, the village and their dwellers, make up the superorganism he was able to become conscious of within himself. Indeed, that overture towards a sacramental dwelling, building and tilling included, as we shall see later on, organizes a set of attitudes that, once incorporated in our mode of being within the world and relating to it, amplifies the possibility of experiencing that suave serenity that stems from being and accepting what one is. Such acceptance implies a tender openness, a curiosity in relation to the other and a methodological effort of anamnesis as well. The metanoic experience of being one with the Whole, of being germane to everything that blooms around us, an experience historically obliterated by the adventitious accumulation of social, political and economic mores, drastically alters our ways of being and relating to reality. To achieve that serenity, a new *ethos* is implied, a new look and a new doing is demanded: a new Ethics.

COSMOS

When one talk about "ethics," one tends to forget the origin of the expression. The Greek language has two very similar words whose meaning, in time, were conflated: one with a short "e" (*epsilon*, "ε," εθοσ): ethos, and another one with a long "e" (*eta*, η, ηθοσ): *ēthos*, whence the word "ethics," "character," or "traditional customs" in Greek. Originally, the word *ēthos* meant a "burrow," the "lair," or the place of reunion of a group of kindred animals. It does not seem to be a coincidence that Thoreau, in meditating on houses and building, states that every house, every human habitation, is nothing more than a "corridor," a "porch," for a burrow: "the house is still but a sort of porch at the entrance of a burrow."[13] For us, here, this relationship of ethos, "character" and ēthos "burrow" is decisive in the amplitude of its reach, since it will unfold in many dimensions along this essay. The expression ēthos, and its most archaic meaning is already attested in Homer,[14] and that nexus ties the epistemic knot of Thoreau's outlook both on "house" and the world as well. The perception that our values derive from our "burrow"—"house"—"habitat," whence we watch the world, informing the nature of our character, seems to signify that what we believe in and how we act is determined by the constitution of our way of dwelling and the place we inhabit. This perspective makes a lot of sense when one remembers that the shared values of a certain human community, its collective character or customs and traditions, in Greek, "ethos," are also forged by our collective natural and cultural habitats and the way we interact with the others in a historical and dialogical tension. This seems to point to the fact that our outlook onto the world is, fundamentally, in its most archaic dimension, the result of the landscape where we flourish and inhabit: our most radicular belonging to our burrow, be it the earth, the trees or a village. Thus, when one speaks of "Ethics," or one defends a certain set of values, what one is in fact doing is transposing to the axiological universe the circumstanciality of one's belonging, of one's "*oikeiosis*." Further, if this equation is correct, our "*óikos*-ēthos," our "home-burrow," must necessarily be expanded to shelter the beings with whom we partake of our common home, our common habitat, creating literally a "common unity," a "community" that necessarily should contemplate our interdependence with the others beings that irrupt in the same horizon as we do, for if Thoreau is correct in affirming that we are part and parcel of Nature, our ultimate axiological identitarian conformation is the result of a myriad of values and drives espoused by the other beings that dwell with us in our circumstantiality, who, together with us, appear amid innumerable processes and phenomena that occur outside and far beyond our supposed free-will. Our singularity, then, seems to be a fluid mosaic of elements acting, reacting and interacting in a certain environment, and our beliefs, it turns out, seem to be the result of a plurality of drives wrapped up in the organic tension between ourselves and the plethora of events that draw the landscape we are rooted in, our circumstantial plot of Nature.

Thus, to dwell or to inhabit means extraordinarily more than just to find oneself thrown in a certain context. One may very well suspect that individuals—inhabitants, indwellers—are basically a modality or the optimum organic and inorganic result of tensions and interactions of their ontological backgrounds, natural and cultural, if one still cares in doing such a distinction. Moreover, as interdependent manifestations of Nature, and going beyond a reflection on our ontological singularity, to meditate on our dwelling from our "homes-burrows," from our "*óikoi-ēthoi*," seems to invite the possibility of replacing a "philosophical anthropology," an attempt of reflecting about the nature of a human being, for a "philosophical ethology," to respect and embrace the beings that flower, with us, amongst multivalent factors, and who manifest themselves in the shared drives and values of a certain habitat, since to embrace non-critically and overvalue an anthropic perspective debases, corrupts and deforms the existential conglomeration of beings, phenomena and processes that compose our existential proximity.

More than just that, to reflect on the way we inhabit our landscape from our ēthoi, our "home-burrow," seems to invite a repositioning of every philosophical anthropology that presupposes a supernatural human nature—be it a soul or reason—that singles us out of Nature. Maybe a good starting-point to that repositioning might be, as I said earlier, the formulation of an anthropological ethology—also derived from ēthos—i.e., an effort of understanding the behaviour and constitution of the human flourishing in a natural, material and immanent perspective, that is, disrobed of any metaphysical extraordinary status whatsoever, which might ascribe to us any sort of cosmic centrality or finality in the concert of all creatures. Thus, to unmask the humans of their transcendent imagined position might help in advancing a new set of values that could anchor what Nietzsche used to call "fidelity to Earth," one of the cervical nerves of Zarathustra's thought. That is why to reposition our look towards the "burrow" might conjure up the elaboration of a new set of values, or a new set of "new tablets," to carry on with the Nietzschean imagery. This new set of cognitive values and methods demand a more sustained reflection. In this light, what follows is an exploration of the possibilities of that ethic-ethological look, a possible new set of tablets to sustain that new "religare" as a necessary "renaturare," that is, the possibility of realizing our most archaic constitution as filaments of consciousness that vascularizes Nature—or the Whole—or, in other words, to be able to awaken to the experience that it is Nature Herself who is trying to achieve self-awareness through us, Her masks. Thence, to imagine another originary locus, above of or outside Nature, for our ultimate identitarian constitution seems to be a deformation of our existential condition. It is important to underline that the anamnetic effort in search of our phenomenal "arché" serves not only as a recognitive tool of our ontological singularity, but as a meditation on the principles that might organize the latent possibilities of an immanent ethics that might advance on the path of a critique of our traditional imperative or transcendental ethical heritage.

As to the first aspect, the anamnetic process as a recognitive tool, I shall have more to say further along the way, when I will try to explore some of the mechanisms utilized by Thoreau to retrieve that experience. Here, suffice it to say that the recognition of our natural belonging is always a feasible and actual possibility, our many ideological layers of civilizational varnish notwithstanding. That the process must necessarily be anamnetic is explained by the fact that it is not the case of acquiring a new nature or a novel capacity, rather, it is fundamentally a matter of rediscovering the uncountable common denominators between ourselves and the natural world. In this sense, proximity to a natural landscape becomes an irreplaceable movement orchestrated by the necessity of leaning and convergence towards Nature, an attempt of developing a reverent intimacy towards Her, as well as the possibility of developing a tender and careful auscultation of the myriad silent choruses that encompass Her multiple domains. Secondly, it follows from the previous string of voices that it appears to be improbable that the retrieving of our most original belonging, our oikeiosis, shall not reorient our values, once rediscovered our old-new "natural sanity." This reset is extremely important.

If the thesis that the constitution of our consciousness, this perennial witness that rarely refluxes or relaxes, and our outermost physicality help shaping our identity and singles us out from the weft of the innumerable beings and phenomena is correct, and if one considers that our values are exhalations of our subjectivity, physicality and surroundings, then one must be prepared to acknowledge the fact that our ethical perspectives are, fundamentally, axiological transpositions, to the realm of the ideological, both of our natural singularity as well as our reactions and interactions with the environment we dwell in. Thus, any "Ethics" that does not take into consideration the other beings that people our immediate horizon, our circumstantiality, meaning, who shape and constitute ourselves as well, is fated to be partial, unilateral and specist. Very much like our incontrollable bio-chemical synapses, if our values in fact represent our most archaic constitution, our outlook/mode of being from our burrow, our natural, elemental rooting, then the layers of societal and civilizational mechanisms of domestication do not translate, as Thoreau untiringly points out, our most essential needs and veritable constitution. On the contrary, our cultural dynamics, in falsifying our nature by advocating a supernatural origin of ourselves, be it through the possession of a supposed "soul" or "reason," procures gratification of its own corrupted and imaginary needs and goals. Our deformation is so spectacular that, as hindu penitents, we have irremediably corrupted our nature. Thoreau writes:

"What I have heard of Brahmins sitting exposed to four fires and looking in the face of the sun; or hanging suspended, with their heads downward, over flames; or looking at the heavens over their shoulders until it becomes impossible for them to resume their natural position, while from the twist of the neck nothing but liquids can pass into the stomach."[15]

Our myopia regarding our true nature deforms both our look on ourselves and on Nature as well, creating the perfect opportunity and justification for Her anthropic subordination and instrumentalization. From our unilateral divorce from Her seems to follow our violence in regarding Nature only as a resource for our hypertrophied consumerist desire, apparently the only redeeming way in search of happiness left in a long-ago disenchanted world. According to him: "almost all man's improvements, so called, as the building of houses, and cutting down of the forest and all large trees, simply deform the landscape, make it more tame and cheap."[16]

To remedy that deformation, i.e., to retrieve our "natural condition," overcoming that supposed metaphysical pedigree and attempting to minor our violent impact on Nature, the anamnetic effort and the realization of the obsolescence of the many specist Ethics so far formulated by our philosophical tradition seem to be inseparable conditions. To reach that profound rooting, that awareness of being Nature and inhabiting Her in a conscious, deliberate manner, it appears to me that the most fecund way of imagining an universalization of the scope of Ethics is to include those whose silenced voices have not been heeded so far, however, it is not our intention to discuss and analyse here the relative merits of anthropocentric, biocentric or any other ethical formulation,[17] rather, our most immediate goal is to formulate a critique of our supposed metaphysical genealogy, the main rationale, I believe, of our hubris against Nature and a necessary condition towards the possibility of rectifying it. As Thoreau famously sings:

"I wish to speak a word for Nature, for absolute freedom and wildness, as contrasted with a freedom and culture merely civil,—to regard man as an inhabitant, or a part and parcel of Nature, rather than a member of society. I wish to make an extreme statement, if so I may make an emphatic one, for there are enough champions of civilization: the minister, and the school-committee and every one of you will take care of that."[18]

To reach the full realization of his/our natural rooting, Thoreau had to embark in an extraordinary self-discovery adventure, caging himself in his hut, under the singing pines, deep inside Nature, by the shores of Walden Pond. It is important to remember that writing, for Thoreau, was not only a creative activity, but a self-knowledge exercise as well. It is not a coincidence that *Walden* first title was "A history of myself," indicating the convergence between creativity (writing, building, tiling), the study of Nature, and self-knowledge. Indeed, there, at Walden, he was able to discover that he was, in fact, Walden, or Nature. Thus, we must underscore the fact that Thoreau is not prepared to speak "about" or "on" Nature anymore, but "for," that is, "on Her behalf" and, much more radically, "as" Nature. By realizing and accepting his true nature and the germane community he shared with his natural companions, all those beings that flourished in his immediacy, Thoreau was able to discard the millennia of cultural/metaphysical indoctrination that lies at the root of the falsifying and deforming processes that christened the human being as a being above and beyond the natural, material and immanent dynamics that constitute our most archaic elemental constitution. In a certain way, though, we are not even prepared to recognize the shifting of perspectives inaugurated by that revolutionary statement, made more than a hundred and fifty years ago. Given its demolishing repercussions, the novelty of the formulation has been very slowly digested by a civilization still mesmerized by the hierarchical status it has bestowed on itself due to the apparent power of manipulating the natural laws and elements. More than just a radical intuition, it may serve as the basis of a new agenda that, for the first time in History, depicts the true place, the true essence of ourselves. It is not the case that Thoreau was the first to formulate the thesis that we are animals—far from it. However, digging deeper inside his own burrow, Thoreau was capable of discovering not only his internal wildernesses as much as his belonging, his "oikeiosis" to a home (oikos) that was not only his: he discovered his common home, his common-unity, his community with the myriad beings and phenomena that informed, constituted and circumscribed his own nature. By rediscovering that "he was Nature," he was able to lend Her his voice or, again, Nature was able to express Her conscious realization of being Herself through him. This ethological self-discovery, both in its ethical and anthropological senses, turned him into a medium through whom Nature might speak up through Her many mute and silenced voices. As we shall see further on, he became bird, muskrat, moss, tree, slave, woman, native American and Walden. He became America, a still young and, according to him, an already corrupted America, who sold and exterminated Her sons and daughters of colour, humans and otherwise. He became the Cosmos because he became what he had always been: Nature, a material continuum pervaded by consciousness that vascularizes the totality of existence, singularized in him.

Thus, from a political perspective, the civil freedoms bestowed by a State, and the idea of a Culture separated from Nature, both ideas embodied in the thesis of a supposed primeval social compact responsible for taking humankind from the State of Nature to Civil Society, could only be risible to him. Leaning more towards Rousseau than Hobbes or Locke, the radical freedom he is talking about invites us not only to take a look, but to "take a walk on our wildside," as the song goes. The wildness one finds in oneself, our interior outbacks, so to speak, are microcosmic instances of the cosmic wilderness we cannot get away from. We are irrevocably condemned to be Nature, Culture being, in this perspective, the fantasy name we humans create to depict the way we inhabit this world. And Thoreau is adamantly clear, as we shall see further on, that "Culture" must be thoroughly watered by Nature, if it wants to persevere. They are indissociable. The cultures that got fossilized beyond redemption perished, that is why, according to him, salvation, either for societies or individuals lies in the wilderness. The belief that the political power is the bestower of freedom—when in fact it is only its corruptor—is a central one to him. Nature, wilderness, is the true locus of freedom. Most certainly, the freedom alluded is not the power to do anything, rather, it is the consciousness that we belong, inextricably, to the big concert of creatures, phenomena and processes, to that everlasting natural cycle of creation and destruction. Our recurrent falsification of reality and of ourselves, viz-a-viz our cosmic status and position, our continuous attempt of disentangling ourselves from the natural lace of light that connects everything, creates an insurmountable gap that tends to be filled in by apathy, neglect and indifference: alienation. We do not recognize ourselves anymore as Nature, we do not recognize ourselves anymore as coparticipants of the natural processes. It is only very few people who can still feel—and hear—the call of the wild:

"While almost all men feel an attraction drawing them to society, few are attracted enough to Nature. In their relation to Nature men appear to me for the most part, notwithstanding their art, lower than the animals. It is not often a beautiful relation, as in the case of the animals. How little appreciation of the beauty of the landscape there is among us! We have to be told that the Greeks called the world κόσμος (cosmos), Beauty, or Order, but we do not see clearly why they did so."[19]

It does not seem to be a coincidence that both Thoreau and Emerson[20] use the Greek word "cosmos" to describe their understanding and perception of the world. Beauty, harmony, order, propriety, all those senses are encapsulated in the expression. Incapacity of perceiving such beauty in the natural arrangements of Nature/Reality—arguably one of our most profound possible experiences—debases and lowers us to the sub-animal stratum, in the worst possible sense of the word: insentience. The comparison is intriguing, since animals and their behavior score high in Thoreau's estimates. Animals seem to have a beautiful relation to Nature, apparently, either because they are not "cultural" beings, or because they know their proper places in the economy of the whole. They do not fight against their nature. They seem to accept, they seem to follow in good order, beautifully, the ordering of existence. Our Culture—our art—falsifies that position. We do not follow suit in Nature. We oppose and fight our natural belonging, we resist and destroy our environment, our common home, our shared burrow. We say "no" to Nature and, by doing so, we say "no" to ourselves. We live in constant strife within and outside of us. We fight ourselves and, thus, we live insentiently, denying ourselves our most precious gift and power, the possibility of experiencing the community of the All, the non-dual unicity of the Whole. In our case, alienated from our true nature, we do not live, we just survive. However, the fact that we are cosmic and sentient beings seems to indicate, according to Thoreau, that the utmost experience for us is, in fact, not only purely "spiritual" in a religious sense, but cognitive and aesthetical as well: to be who one is and to be able to appreciate it. Knowledge and beauty, to be and do good and beauty, or, as the greeks used to say: *kalós ka ágathos*. Hence the novelty and power of Thoreau's statement, in speaking as Nature: the importance of a wild look, a look that overcomes our "cattlelicism," the sclerotic set of inherited false beliefs about ourselves and Nature. The embracing of the wildness proposed shall be amplified later, in the larger frame of thinking about Thoreau's strategies to achieving that profound unity with Nature. Here, suffice it to point to some aspects that shall mark, like milestones, the path towards that serene eudaimonia.

The idea of landscape, that mix of subjective and objective components, is central to Thoreau's thought. More than just an aesthetical appeal, the landscape is, in fact, the place one inhabits. To dwell in a certain landscape, we have just said, seems to point to a set of factors that determine both the way one behaves and helps determining the other components of the landscape as well. Such a dialectical tension is orchestrated by the myriad phenomena that compose the horizon towards which one converges within the fluid landscapes. The overture, the openness that every landscape offers, suggests a range of possibilities and combinations. The wilder the landscape, the richer the possibilities of experiencing that unicity for, unmediated by civilization or society mores, one can feel the upsurge of the sap that roots one to a certain natural setting, to a still little deformed landscape. Moreover, that sap is the very same one that feeds the woods, stones, beasts, brooks and ponds. No more jailed inside the golden cage of our proud and splintering subjectivity that excises ourselves from the natural continuum of the wilderness, Thoreau is able to embody and record the experience of being an interdependent organic conscious filament of the eternally recurrent cycles of Nature, the creative and destructive drives that operate inside and outside of himself. Associated with the infinite creatures that share the landscape with him, that non-dual belonging re-establishes the optimum pre-lapsarian condition of our exile from the natural community, from the tender—and sometimes necessarily violent—intimacy that dissolves the fluid borders of ontic limits, those imaginary perspectival blunders that our inattentive coups d'oeil register when we do not stop to meditate serenely on the nature of beings, making us commit the mistake of trying to understand ourselves from a supposed autarchic atomism that severs us from the surrounding concert of phenomena. This circumstantial sphere of the natural/wild landscape where Thoreau was rooted is rarely experienced, for we have been trained to ignore and distance ourselves from that wilderness, both interior and exterior, relegating to oblivion the supressed intrinsic richness of that original openness: we have become sedentary in more than one way.

By returning to Nature, the animal Thoreau was able to be fed once again by the sap that spiked his rooting in his burrow/hut at Walden Pond. There, he could dive into the translucent turquoise waters which dissolved every imaginary membrane that separated him from the elemental re-union that formed both his singularity as well as circumstantiality. In this perspective, Thoreau's digging/building of his burrow/hut at Walden mirrors, in a reflexive and seminal fashion, an ethical, ethological, economic and a political project that will constitute the kernel of his glance towards the world. Later in life, after leaving Walden Pond and returning to Concord, Thoreau is going to realize that, in fact either at Walden or in Concord, he, Thoreau, is just Nature observing, groping, knowing Herself through one of Her conscious filaments, himself. Cape Cod or the village of Concord, it is exactly the same Nature operating, with the negative proviso that when one forgets of that non-duality and engages in a fundamental dichotomy of separating oneself from Nature, the essential Other, deformation occurs.

Thus, it is in this way, as an in-dweller of the wildernesses of his soul and of his senses, in constant dialogue with the ancients, as well as with the moss and flowers that flourished under his feet, that he will inhabit his burrow-world, from where he is going to observe, sing and celebrate his beloved "Maiden." Through his pioneering, idiosyncratic and singular glance in relation to Nature, Thoreau broke with millennia-old metaphysical view of a supernatural human being, preparing the terrain for new philosophical seeds to be sowed on the ample breast of Gaia. By displacing our anthropic centrality in the universe, by breaking with the monochord string of his contemporary Christianity, Thoreau reaches a new plateau, with ampler, richer vistas. By perceiving himself to be leaf, stone, moss, wood and beast, he reinaugurates a new relationship with Nature, a closer, more tender one, than the ones his fellow human beings had previously had. It is not that Thoreau was embracing the end of the violent appropriation of Nature's fruits, but with him it was reduced to a bare minimum, since, as he was very much aware of, violence belongs intrinsically in Nature. Hunting, fishing: Thoreau had a good word to say about those activities, our hubris being the unnecessary and unnatural craving for accumulation, as his mantra spelt: simplicity, simplicity, simplicity. The reorientation of his needle towards the ancients, instead of the promises sung by the sirens of the Industrial Revolution and organized capitalism, his inward look and his going to the woods instead of the market, his befriending of the native American and the slaves as well as the white intelligentsia by whom he was surrounded in Concord, "the Transcendental" capital of the United States, points to a cosmopolitanism that, if never explicitly articulated, may be deduced by its many instantiations. Even when confronting with acidity the social mores of his community, Thoreau never lost sight of his Humanism, understood in its classical sense. We tend to forget that the lighthouse of his inner visions became beams that helped to reveal a new world, visions so powerfully enlightening that they would illuminate Gandhi, Matin Luther King, Jr., and countless others in their struggle against human exploitation, humiliation and savagery against humankind and Nature. By being himself—sincerely, authentically—he helped reshaping the world. However, before we progress any further, it is important to remember that his views on Nature were far, very far from a source of romantic delight with the wild landscapes or any form of escapism to an arcadian long-lost primitive haven. The embracing of the elements that inhabit in a still radicular bond with Nature, be it plants, animals, native populations, served a higher purpose: to contrast them with a sclerotic society, an industrial and imperial America, corrupted by slavery and consumerism. An acid critic of his contemporary America, inauthentic and insincere, it was in his solitary communion with the golden contrast of the blue and green of the woods that he belonged and dwelt. It was there that he found his source and burrow, his repose and renovation. However, Nature, to him, was far from being a calm, pacific or idyllical locus. Nature could be terrible, horrendous and frightening as well. The destructive billows that surged on the emerald back of New England's ocean confided terrible and furious secrets to him, as it vomited corpses on the beaches of Cape Cod because of the shipwreck of the brig St. John. There, and elsewhere, Thoreau would savour Nature's *mysterium tremendum et fascinans*, Her fury, desolation and destruction. At Mount Ktaad, an ancient Amerindian holy place, he could experience the hardness and the indifference of the natural world towards us, always indifferent by our praises, prayers and tears. As our loving mother and our cruel hanger nothing could be further from Thoreau's conception of Nature than a romantic idyllic venue to stroll around. No. Violent death and a frenetic bubbling of life, a continuous orgy of creation and destruction, flourishing in continuous transformation, moderated by Her rhythmic cycles, might be a more apt image. It is this sort of landscape that we must be prepared to meet as we start our adventurous promenade through Thoreau's Nature. An unknown pathway yet, paradoxically, much nearer to us than anything else. For Thoreau, it started in Concord, and ended up in the Cosmos for, by truly being the former, he became the latter. However, one may very well ask here: "if we are really Nature, isn't our Culture, and the totality of its characteristics, a manifestation of Nature? Isn't this the way society—natural society-is supposed to be?" To answer that question, we have to go back in time and place. More exactly, to ancient Athens, to watch a tragedy by Aeschyllus.

NOTES

1. Thoreau, H. D. *Walden*, Princeton: Princeton University Press, 1971, p. 3.
2. *Walden*, p. 72–79.
3. *Walden*, p. 6.
4. *Walden*, p. 90.
5. *Walden*, p. 133.
6. Oikeiois is a Greek word derived from *Óikos*, "home," whence both "economy" and "ecology" come. The word *Oikeiosis* is generally translated as "belonging," "familiarity," and made its first appearance in the history of philosophy with the stoics, who used the term to justify some of their epistemological and cognitive perspectives. Here, we shall use it in the sense of "belonging" and "familiarity" with ones environment.
7. According to Emerson's Funeral Eulogy Of Thoreau.
8. *Walden*, p. 138.
9. Thoreau, H. D. *A Week on the Concord and Merrimack Rivers, Walden, The Maine Woods*, and *Cape Cod*. New York: The Library Of America, 1985, p. 851.
10. In fact, his baptism name, which happened on October 12th of the same year, was David Henry Thoreau. Later in life Thoreau would invert the order of his name to Henry David Thoreau.
11. *Walden* p. 100–103.
12. *A Week on the Concord and Merrimack Rivers*, p. 350.
13. *Walden*, p. 45.
14. *Iliad* VI. 511; XV, 268, "The Burrow of an Animal," "The Habitats of Horses," and "*Ethea Hippon*." There are two words for *Ethos* in Greek, one with an *Eta* (Hθoσ) and one with *Epsilon* (Eθoσ).
15. *Walden*, p. 4.

16. Thoreau, H. D. *Collected Essays and Poems*. The Library Of America, Vol. 124. New York: The Library Of America, 2001 (Henceforth: Name Of The Poem/ Essay *CEP*, Page Number). *Walking*, p. 230.

17. For a good general introduction to the many strands of ethics available concerning the issues I am discussing here, a good place to start might be *Environmental Ethics: The Big Questions*, Edited by David R. Keller. Chichester: Wilye-Blackwell, 2010.

18. *Walking, CEP*, p. 225.

19. *Idem*, p. 251.

20. Emerson, R. W. *Essays And Lectures*. New York: The Library Of America, vol. 15, 1983, p. 14.

Chapter 2

The Long Shadow of Prometheus
Civilization and Alienation

"Nor brick-woven dwellings Knew they, placed in the sun, nor wood-work; but digging down they dwelt, like puny Ants, in sunless nooks of caves . . . understand, all arts to mortals from Prometheus."[1] Aeschylus' "Prometheus bound," one of Thoreau's most important translations, offers a remarkable opportunity to reflect on the relationship between Nature and technique; more than a simple translation, Thoreau seems to have been deeply impacted not only by Aeschylus' aesthetical force, but also by the contents of his tragedies, apparently turning them into a programmatic source of reflection as well. Another play of Aeschylus, also translated by Thoreau, "Seven against Thebes,"[2] with its eulogy of heroes, an important concept for both writers, and its richly crafted mythopoetic language suggests that the Greek playwright was among Henry's constant intellectual companions, if one is to judge by Thoreau's lavishing praise.[3]

The tension between Nature and technique, the latter being one of the pillars of every culture/society, is a recurring theme in Thoreau's writings. The centrality of that tension is so evident that one might risk affirming it is one of the leitmotifs of his work. However, Thoreau's plea for a more profound connection with Nature and his denunciation of society notwithstanding, a deep ambiguity regarding the nature, relevance and uses of technique/technology may be easily detected in his work. Moreover, his impassioned defense of the "sacramental" usage of some techniques—agriculture and building immediately come to mind—makes that tension one of the most difficult problems to unravel in his thought,[4] his privilege of the mythopetic linguistic register instead of a logocentric articulation adding further depth to the issue. Further still, if one bears in mind that such a tension between Nature and Technique is ultimately the cause of our alienation from the consciousness of our own natural ontological belonging, with its myriad of disagreeable consequences, meticulously pointed out by him throughout his works, the problem assumes a decisive role and becomes a plausible point of departure to a critical appraisal of his views on Culture, Nature, Technique as well as his goals and methods. Thus, in the next pages, I will try to address that issue, first, detecting and reflecting over some of the many modes of alienation which Thoreau delineates from his acute observation of the lives of his contemporaries; then, I shall proceed to endeavor to isolate the cause of those ills: an unconscious appropriation of Nature through an instrumentalization of technology that distances us from Her and that, ultimately, crystallizes into an alienated and artificial society which produces and reproduces insincere and alienating values. So, in a sense, I shall mirror Thoreau's and the proverbial "philosophical-medical" simile methodology: starting with the symptomatology, a set of ingrained beliefs, practices and behaviors that entail the existential pains we are so much prone to; further on, try to detect the origin of such set of symptomatological phenomena. Only then we shall be equipped to deal with the administration of the proper medicine: what I have named "Pedagogy of awakening," for, if Philosophy is in fact the medicine of the soul, as many of the ancients affirmed, awakening to the nature and origins of our illnesses, taking the proper medicine and, ideally, curing the illness becomes the optimum conclusion of its therapeutic process.[5] In other words, in terms of program, our immediate plan is to detect: (i) what is the problem, (ii) the wherefore of the problem, so that we can see how Thoreau tries to (iii) remedy it. Further on, in Chapter 3, I shall explore the concept of "sacramental technique," that is, the possibility of transforming, by using it in a sacramental way, our relationship to technique and its role in Thoreau's "Pedagogy of awakening."

The very first pages of Thoreau's *Walden*[6] paint a grim picture of the condition of humankind in general and of his fellow Concordians in particular: insincere, pathetic and painful lives of quite and not so "quiet desperation."[7] Distant from Nature and drowning in society's degenerate and inauthentic mores, we live, according to the Chanticleer of Concord, in more than one sense, on another's brass, "aes alienum,"[8] the brass in question being society's sclerotic and coagulated spiritual, social, political and economic inherited spurious values. The result of this rather miserable situation is, according to Thoreau, the monochordic and maddening societal "cattlelicism" which most people embrace, instead of searching for one's authenticity, the consciousness of one's singularity that, ideally, according to his perspective, would rend each and every one of us a happier and better human being, besides building a healthier society. Sometimes dangerously verging on a rather disagreeable homiletic high moral tone, something Thoreau himself deplores in his own writings,[9] we shall see that four very interesting and important points will emerge from the ghastly pen picture of his denunciations: (i) Thoreau does not seem to contemplate the possibility that people are or can be very happy in their situation; (ii) He also does not seem to question his supposedly privileged own high moral ground—a recurrent trace in his, sometimes, overly judgemental writings; (iii) He is also apparently convinced that their situation is a matter of choice, which, by the way, underlies his vacillation between free-will and determinism[10] and—finally the good news—(iv) our mistakes are of an epistemological, and not an ontological nature: in plain English, we suffer, according to him, miserably, because we are wrong or/and lazy, not because we are bad, another typical instance where his Greek intellectual heritage overcomes his Christian upbringing surroundings. Leaving aside (i), (ii) and (iii) for the time being (they will return later on), I would like to detain myself a bit more here on (iv).

"Men labor under a mistake."[11] Exploring the double semantic use that "labor" implies, Thoreau seems to suggest that our mistake is actually a double one: we not only work in a mistaken way[12] as far as—always according to him—our vital supposed priorities and necessities are concerned, our goals are wrong, but also that very mistaken way of laboring towards that set of unfortunate goals originates from laboring under a mistake, i.e., we operate under an epistemological malfunction that, once rectified, would ideally open up the possibility of embarking on a more meaningful and satisfying life: bottom line, we make poor choices because we do not understand things correctly. As the mainstream Greek ethical tradition (Socratic-Platonic-Aristotelian-Hellenistic) says, nobody makes a bad choice—or a mistake, for that matter—willingly; once one is shown a better goal and the best way to achieve it, one would automatically mend one's way. Thoreau seems to fully subscribe to that thesis. Now, that is a very significant claim. Thoreau is actually saying that not only our goals, our "ends," in his peculiar Aristotelian-Christian vocabulary[13] are unfortunate, but he also seems to be implying that our cognitive blunders, whose origins may be ascribed part to individual nature and part to a dysfunctional societal diseducation, are potentially amendable, as his formal stints as a revolutionary teacher, together with other contemporaries educators like Bronson Alcott, Emerson *et al* attest, but, more importantly, there is always the possibility of correcting, through a new paideia, both the ends and the means of individuals and societies as well. That would certainly call for a complete reversal of society's educational project, as his traumatic official teaching experience shows,[14] but, failing that, there is also the possibility of a private, particular self-education, a therapeutic self-care based on a set of practices that Thoreau is happy to share with us.[15] With that in mind, it is time now to delve into the muddy waters of individuals' and society's misfortunes.

"*The twelve labors of Hercules were trifling in comparison with those which my neighbors have undertaken; for they were only twelve, and had an end.*"¹⁶ Again, labors; again, mythology. For such a hardworking man as Thoreau certainly was, the mention of "labor"—most types of them, but not all of them—comes suspiciously close to a negative adjective. When in search of images to compare the lives of his contemporaries, the only ones that he comes up with are extraordinarily painful: the penitences of Indian ascetics, contemporary slavery, the labors of Hercules. All of them brutal, unfortunate and, ultimately, tragic: the Indian ascetics, the Brahmins—from India or Boston—deform irreversibly their bodies and minds; black slaves' average lives were abysmally short with its multiple attending indignities and Hercules ended up mad killing his wife and children. For someone brought up within a protestant work ethic environment, Thoreau seems happily oblivious to its merits. Indeed, his deliberate emphasis on leisure, inaction, both spiritually[17] and materially, are recurrent throughout his writings and form a prerequisite to pursuing humankind's higher ends. Misguided hard work deforms, numbs and obliterates our most delicate and spiritual potentialities. Now, such misguided hard work is fundamentally connected to the need to work according to poor choices that stem from artificial and unnecessary values that become ingrained in a dysfunctional and sclerotic society. A society Thoreau sometimes believes to be beyond redemption, despairing to see that it is foolish enough to condemn itself to a perpetual condition of spiritual anguish, political alienation and economic debt. A society Thoreau is only too happy to escape whenever possible, escape that comes to a rupture point when, on July 4th 1843, he moves to his cabin, declaring his autarky and autonomy in relation to an appalling corrupt society, tainted by its allegiance to an enslaving, belligerent and imperialist state, and (mis)guided by an unfair and oppressive economic model that was based on a budding mechanization and industrialization that instrumentalizes technology to obscurantist ends.

Given Concord's agriculture-based economy, farmers and farming mores, beliefs and practices become the immediate available values for his sustained scathing analysis. "Serfs of the soil, machines,"[18] he likens them, "through mere ignorance and mistake, are so occupied with the factitious care and superfluously coarse labors of life that its finer fruits cannot be plucked by them."[19] Ignorance, mistake, coarse labors are key words here and their equation is inescapable: ignorance, mistake, suffering. *In nuce*: humankind suffers not because it is bad but because they are mistaken about what true good is. It is hardly possible to be more Socratic than that . . . worryingly, the list of our shortcomings is far from over. The attack goes on and on, but we shall skip the most vicious blows: "it is evident what mean and sneaking lives many of you live . . . lying, flattering, voting . . . talk of divinity in man! . . . The mass of men lead lives of quiet desperation."[20] "Poor things, those Concordians!," anyone with a shred of a heart may sympathetically moan. Against their most cherished values, young Henry's whetted look is hard and merciless.

However, it is from the hardness and mercilessness of the look that comes the possibility of applying the healing balm. In the rhetorically remarkable passage that follows, Thoreau remonstrates: "When we consider what, to use the words of the catechism, is the chief end of man, and what are the true necessities and means of life, it appears as if men had deliberately chosen the common mode of living because they preferred it to any other. Yet they honestly think there is no choice left."[21] Brushing aside again the issue of free will for a moment, the passage is extraordinarily important, both rhetorically and substantially: it marks the climax of the symptomatology and the beginning of the examination of our mistakes' origins, later on to be articulated in terms of an explicit possible alternative to that crushing mass of woes that infested Concordian bodies, hearts, minds and souls. It is important to underline the fact that it is here that some of Thoreau's key concepts are introduced and they will, in a very clear sense, delineate the contours of the perimeter of Thoreau's reflection in *Walden*: "the end of men," "their true necessities" and "the best way of life: our lives" finality, the meaning of our existence, and the necessary means towards achieving that end. The Chanticleer of Concord is now ready to start his cock a doodle doo.

What is the end of individuals? Why do I, you and everyone else exist? Is there any finality? In case there is, what is the *telos*, the finality, of individual humans, to use Aristotle's original concept?[22] That is the most important question Thoreau raises to create the conditions of possibility to developing his "Pedagogy of awakening." What is the rationale of our flourishing into existence? Why we are the way we are? Why do we live the way we do, or considering a possible alternative, what should we live for and how should we live to achieving that end. These are the questions that Thoreau is going to tackle, and based on his experience, reflect on the possibilities of curing both the sick individual and the sick society.

In more than one sense *Walden* is a cultivator almanac. Written in a *chiaroscuro* technique[23] so that its contours may help better delineate the picture he is painting, it also became an undying ode to Walden Pond, the place: an enchanted spot for the cultivation of the soil, for the cult of Nature and for self-culture; cultivator, cultivation, cult, culture: the many hues of the Latin verb *colere* seem to be central to Thoreau's project. *Colere*, "to cultivate" in Latin, spells more precisely tender care, constant attention and sustained effort, all important bearings on Thoreau's topography of the way to wisdom, and constitute, undoubtedly, his favored set of tools to approach reality. It is there, at Walden, that he will have the necessary leisure to write and think about the good life, the eudaimonic promise of spiritual dawn that energizes his efforts throughout his life. Given the prolonged reflection on these matters in its pages, we will take *Walden* as our guide to understand that project of Nature cultivation, contemplation and self-culture, Thoreau's personal alternative to the sorry spiritual and social state of his fellow contemporaries. In this light, *Walden* encapsulates and becomes an astonishing answer to Emerson's challenge *"Gnothi sauton and study Nature,"* that is, "know thyself and meditate on our most archaic belonging," two clearly interconnected imperatives.

The possibility of living sincerely, authentically, becomes nothing less than an obsession for Thoreau, a man in quest of creating the conditions to accepting and cultivating his singularity, contrasted with what he believed to be a cattle's life, his contemporaries own poor alternative. Highlighting that he did not want to give advice to those brave souls who are capable of minding their own business, those "strong and valiant natures,"[24] the target group of his whetted look and recipients of his wisdom was to be composed by his contemporary unenlightened New Englanders, the "Johnathans," as he calls them. If the ultimate goal of Philosophy is to teach us how to lead better lives in a practical way,[25] as a philosopher—and I fully assume that Thoreau is convinced of his philosophical role as a "doctor of the soul"—the very first question to be asked is: "what is their real condition?" Amplifying his case-study, "what is humankind's real condition?" According to him, decadent, degenerate, alienated, suffering. That would be the diagnosis; however, Thoreau goes on in his analysis: is this a situation, a condition, or is it its true nature? Indeed, he seems to believe that the human potential appears to be quite another one: awakened, wise. The assessment necessarily begs the question: How does such a fall become possible? How come from such a lofty potential we plummet into such existential quagmire? Going beyond an immediate and facile Rousseauism, notwithstanding the fact that both share a number of views, Thoreau starts his genealogical effort to trace our individual and societal dysfunction by a critique of the inherited "wisdom," the coagulated experience of the past generations that tends to solidify in prohibitive mores and stupid prejudices: "it is never too late to give up our prejudices . . . what old people say you cannot do you try and find you can. Old deeds for old people and new deeds for new . . . practically the old have no very important advice to give the young . . . I have lived some thirty years on this planet, and I have yet to hear the first syllable of valuable or even earnest advice from my seniors."[26] Thoreau's rude dismissal of his elders' "wisdom" should be put in the correct perspective, since it is a necessary demand of the anamnetic process towards awakening to deconstruct the invalid and preposterous catalogue of inherited and ingrained prejudices. However, the first thing that is important to remember, I believe, is Thoreau's profound love and respect for ancient wisdom and archaic cultures. It is not past opinions themselves that are bad, it is a sort of past opinions that should be shunned; as he says elsewhere: "it is fit that the past should be dark; though the darkness is not so much a quality of the past, as of tradition."[27] Thus, the basic problem is not the whole of society's axiological inheritance, but a very specific set of values that obfuscate the intrinsic richness of individual creativity and singularity. The very first step towards the opportunity of redeeming us from our numbing slumber, in other words, is the necessity of discarding the values that crystallize as "truth": morally, a social consensus that prevents the possibility of change, either individually or collectively; "scientifically," as an insurmountable, unquestionable "scientific" dogma. Hence it becomes clear Thoreau's condemnation of every inherited "truth," of each "public opinion," that implies, according to Nietzsche, "private laziness."[28] The logical result of this inability to construe one's own outlook towards life, "this untried experiment,"[29] can only be a degrading alienation, fruit of the acritical acceptance of society's morals and values. Worse, whenever one embraces a view that is not the result of a particular discovery, an unfolding of one's own perspective, not only one does collapse to the level of cattle, but one helps to reinforce the impossibility of dissent, becoming a docile instrument in the enacting of the collective paralyzing ideological totalitarianism over the potentialities that lie hidden in every individual. Not only does one fall sick, obliterating one's original natural "healthy" condition,[30] but one becomes a passive vector, instrumental in contaminating society with the rabid virus of "cattlelicism." Therefore, it makes a lot of sense to his pedagogic anamnetic therapy for Thoreau to affirm the methodological relevance of the apophatic deconstruction of value-negative laden cultural debris, in order to level and clean the field up for further potential liberative gnoseological building. Different from building a house, as we shall soon note, the building of a free human being or a society is—due to the already sorry state of affairs we find ourselves in—in fact, a rebuilding; first must come the demolition, so that one can build over a new base, this time, ideally, a "sacramental" one.[31]

Spiritual and moral alienation, to make matters slightly worse, also have their painful material correlates: socio-political and economic dysplasia. According to Thoreau, the State dehumanizes most of its citizens:

"The mass of men serve the state thus, not as men mainly, but as machines, with their bodies. They are the standing army, and the militia, jailers . . . in most cases there is no free exercise whatever of the judgement or of the moral sense; but they put themselves on a level with wood and earth and stones; and wooden men can perhaps be manufactured that will serve the purpose as well. Such command no more respect than men of straw or a lump of dirt. They have the same sort of worth only as horses and dogs . . . very few, as heroes, patriots, martyrs, reformers in the great sense, and men (Thoreau's emphasis), serve the state with their consciences also, and so necessarily resist it for the most part."[32]

Given Thoreau's basic belief that the human being is part and parcel of Nature,[33] it is intriguing that he has never attempted to articulate a theory about the natural development of the State as most political writers have done, in many hues of the so-called social compact.[34] The debate about the origins of the State is a fascinating one but, unfortunately, we cannot go that way here, however, it is important to note Thoreau's statement that a citizen's true role is, sometimes, to check the totalitarianism of the State. Once again, the individual stance of dissent is the exception to the general rule. Such a heroic behavior, exemplified by Thoreau himself in his refusal to contribute to what he perceived as an imperialist annexation of part of Mexico's territory and his consequent arrest, can be compared to Antigone's role, when she defies the law of the State. It is a classic example of the conflict between Natural Law and State Law.[35] As we know, Thoreau sided with Antigone and Natural law.

"If I should draw a long breath in the neighborhood of these institutions, their weak and flabby sides would fall out."[36] Basically, being excessively reductionist, to Thoreau, Society is sick, bad and Nature is healthy, good. Society's institutions may be seen as a set of instruments whose ultimate goal are to goad individuals towards conformism and submission to the State: "men are degraded when considered as the members of a political organization . . . in society you will not find health, but in nature . . . society is always diseased, and the best is most so."[37] Is it surprising that he did not get many invitations to dine out? Considered collectively, humans are simply vectors of society's many diseases. An individual is degraded and debased when not examined in its singularity and authenticity, since society's "cattlelicism," its herd nature, is anathema to Thoreau's rugged individualism. The permanent tension between individual liberty and law creates a situation where the dystopic State, instead of creating the conditions for the flourishing of individuals,[38] creates an ideological consensus where apparent security and prosperity assume the central role. If, just for the sake of argument, we understand the State as a political-juridical entity that monopolizes the creation and enforcement of law through "legitimate" violence, and the monopoly to coin currency as well, whose justifications come through a set of ideological mechanisms, we can see that Thoreau's critiques undermine the very foundations of such institution. Such an impasse between freedom and the law, though, it is important to be highlighted, is one of the perennial issues of Political Philosophy and even in the most advanced democratic and liberal societies the tension remains in embers, just to flare spectacularly from times to times. This is only one of the reasons, another one being his distaste for party politics in general, his extraordinarily important Political writings notwithstanding, why it is difficult to pin-point with precision where Thoreau might stand within the current available political spectrum, authors tending to allocate his allegiances from an individualistic republicanism to anarchism through most shades of liberalism. Again, as in most other fields of inquiry with Thoreau, one should hesitate to tying him to any fast and final position, a nuanced view being more adequate for, moreover, the fact that he himself does not differentiate precisely "State" from government and society being yet another reason, or problem, in his thought.[39]

Yet, if Politics may leave some doubt as to where Thoreau stands, in Economics there is no such risk. His mantra "simplicity, simplicity, simplicity"[40] to most problems assumes a central role when discussing Economy, the preliminary issue to be solved if one is to be able to lead "the good life." In fact, this is such an important subject it that does not allow "to be treated with levity,"[41] being at the forefront of his concerns, so much so that it names the first chapter of Walden and is, necessarily, a prerequisite towards creating the conditions of possibility to the afore said "Pedagogy of awakening." His contemporary—and here his criticism is atemporal—and most historical societies too, with the exception of the very few individuals who became for some reason wise, have indulged, unpardonably, in a grotesque consumerism, a necessary result of humans' inability to differentiate the necessities of life from the superfluous ones, whose corollary becomes a particular abomination to Thoreau: luxury.

Luxury is the most singular and immediate sign of downfall not only of individuals but of States, societies and empires as well.[42] In fact, it is the exact material counterpart of spiritual and social disgraces. Like his contemporaries Karl Marx and Friedrich Engels, Thoreau has a lot to say about industrialization, mechanization and their impact on society and individuals. From the more social explicit critique of economic exploitation, the denunciation of the sorry condition of workers, poor salaries, speculative capital, monetization, immigrant work force and its local impact, to the most practical possible education in Economics, instead of the academic syllabi that contain Adam Smith, Say, Ricardo but "irretrievably lead students' parents to bankruptcy," Thoreau develops an extremely acute analysis of contemporary capitalism that serves the double need of being both an important reminder of capitalism's worst excesses as well as being the basis of his pedagogical itinerary. Moreover, from a programmatic philosophical perspective, his views on the economical basics for a happy life are redolent of Epicure's[43] distinction between what is natural and necessary, natural and unnecessary and artificial and unnecessary.[44] To sum it up, Thoreau states that our real "necessaries of life" are: food, shelter, clothing and fuel;[45] when Thoreau squeezes and presses those four basic needs even further, what turns up is the very interesting concept of *heat*, the singular goal of our material existence.[46] Leaving aside for the time being the necessary ascetical nature of those necessaries, it is from those nuclei of life that Thoreau will build a net of arguments that shall lead, ultimately, to the development of his reformative efforts, from the most material to the most spiritual ones, always sensible to the deep connections between them. Further, it is from the need to answer for those necessaries: food, shelter, clothing and fuel—heat—that stems the singular event that shapes and determines our lives and, to a great extent, is responsible for our alienation from Nature: the mastering of the techniques, arguably, the single most important factor in the constitution of historical societies. But to understand that, we must return to the personage who is responsible for such a cataclysmic event: Prometheus.

"Every art of humankind comes from Prometheus," humankind's depressed benefactor himself tells us in *Prometheus bound*.[47] An isolated figure in a desolate place, bound to a rock in the outback of Scythia, far beyond the ecumene, the smartest of the Titans laments his terrible fate. Son of Japetus by the nymph Eurymedon, he had three brothers: Epimetheus, Atlas and Menoetius. After Zeus's rebellion against his father Cronus, Prometheus and Epimetheus sided with Zeus while Atlas and Menoetius sided with Cronus. After Zeus's victory with an outstanding help from Prometheus, the now supreme God punished Atlas and Menoetius and rewarded Prometheus and Epimetheus. Many problems followed, however: Prometheus' worst and unforgivable crime, to steal the fire and all the crafts from the Gods and bestow them upon us, was in fact his second felony, the first being his cheating off the Gods, especially Zeus, during a sacrifice, again benefiting humankind. Justice, this time, though, was swift. He was harshly punished by far-seeing and far-feared Zeus.[48] His justice was not only swift, it was extreme: Prometheus, the fountainhead of all human technology, our very maker, according to some mythological traditions, was to have his liver eaten eternally by a vulture while being scorched during the day by the sun and frozen all night long, the eternal exposure to the elements of Nature appealing to Zeus as an appropriate and maliciously ironic punishment for a traitor who taught us the techniques that safeguard us from Nature Herself and allow us to explore Her. It is symptomatic that a despondent god Hephaestus—Olympian technique itself incarnated—harassed by Power (*Kratos*) and Force (*Bia*), Zeus' minions overseeing Hephaestus' hapless job of binding a relative and fellow craftsman who is to suffer the most abject and unending humiliations, can only half-heartedly accomplish his mission, the same Hephaestus who was robbed, together with Pallas Athena, of his prerogative as master craftsman of gods and humans by the wily Prometheus.

The myth is known from many sources, and Plato's retelling of the tale in his *Protagoras*[49] helps us to better understand the implications and complications of the myth that fascinated Thoreau. According to Plato, Zeus had dispatched the two brothers to oversee the distribution of gifts to Zeus' creatures. Epimetheus (literally, "the one who thinks after," "afterthought"), unfortunately, as his name suggests, made a mess out of it. He gave many excellent gifts to the many beings of creation, but when humankind turn came, there was no gift left. Prometheus ("the one who thinks ahead, beforehand," "forethought"), worried that we might not survive due to our frailty, tricked the two Olympian Gods connected with crafts and techniques, Athena and Hephaestus, and brought down the fire and all other crafts and techniques to us. As we saw, Zeus harsh punishment followed, not before Epimetheus blows it all over again by opening Pandora's box. As we all also know, chaos ensues, hope becoming our last rope.

Prometheus, the "prescient," the one who sees, the one who analyzes and projects, who calculates before he acts, is the prototype of the technician. He is the prototypical engineer, the architect, the one who foresees the problems and tries to solve them, the eponymous troubleshooter who got into a lot of troubles himself. It is important here to point to the fact that, as his name implies, the immediacy of the awareness of the thought process, the cultivation and deliberation of instrumental reason, i.e., the conscience of thought as a mediating tool, marks the anticipating nature of technique: "first they had eyes but had no eyes to see, and ears and heard not. Like shapes within a dream they dragged through their long lives and muddled all haphazardly . . . they did all this without intelligence . . . until it was I that showed them—yes, it was I . . . and letter combinations that hold all in memory."[50] As Prometheus sings his blues, it becomes increasingly clear the progressive complexification of our nature and trajectory in terms of the origins of technical prowess: (i) consciousness, sentience; (ii) language; (iii) technique. This sequence is extremely important. It founds the very basic prerequisites that characterize our own natural, human identity as a singular existential other from the rest of natural beings, with their supposed lack of self-awareness, language and technique and, paradoxically, as a typical mixed blessing, it already marks the very first distancing of ourselves from non-human Nature. Sentiency, in us dubbed as consciousness, the self-awareness of thoughts, those mental events with propositive content which can be conveyed through language: language—our very first tool and, like every other tool, pregnant of promises and dangers.

Albeit embedded in this mythological framework, Thoreau's sophisticated and nonetheless ambiguous reflections on the nature of technique are intriguing. To extricate meaning from such ambiguity one has to be sensitive, I guess, to the fact that, on the one hand, he excoriates most new technologies, vituperating in unequivocal terms against their irrelevance, inopportunity and redundancy: "How little do the most wonderful modern inventions detain us. They insult nature. Every machine, or particular application, seems a slight outrage against universal laws."[51]

On the other hand, he has some of the most sublime words to describe some techniques, Science related ones in general and building and tilling specifically. Assessing profoundly such ambiguity, unfortunately, lies far beyond the scope of this essay, however, there is no dodging the issue, since it lies at the very heart of his project, for it is technique, or better, its mastering, the foundation on which the very concept of Culture resides, that seems to offer the key to understanding the problems of that alienated human life who does not recognize herself as Nature. Rather, instead of lingering on the impasses of that tension in Thoreau, I have opted to stress the unforeseen unfoldings of technique, since it is the mastering of some crafts and techniques that allows us to shift from a nomadic, fluid, sauntering state of existence in the time-space grid to the sedentarian mode of life, which, as I shall argue in the next pages, is responsible for our apparently unavoidable historic process of domestication, whose consequences are individual and collective spiritual, moral, social and economic sclerosis. Such taming of our wild natures, which some anthropologists and historians ascribe to the agricultural revolution that inaugurated what was to be called the Neolithic Era some 10,000 years ago,[52]—undeniably necessary to the construction of civilization as we know it—might be also likened, to continue in the sphere of myth, to be the rupture point from our pre-lapsarian idyllic existence in a bygone Eden to the strife and pains of our cultural and communal existence.

According to Henry—and one can still hear the groan: "Men have become the tools of their tools."[53] This statement is extraordinarily pregnant with meaning. By characterizing our transformation into implements, Thoreau points with precision to the alienating dynamics involved in an unconsidered usage of the myriad implements created by the techniques. Just like owing something transforms one in proprietor of something, that very owning of something binds one in its possessive bond, making oneself a propriety of one's appropriations: one turns into an appropriative being. One is, henceforth, not only a human being anymore, that is, a mode of Nature, but one becomes a juridical and political operative of the social imperative of possessive appropriation of Nature, with its many ideological implications. That transformation of one's ontological nature into a coparticipant of the appropriative model of relating to Nature deforms, necessarily, our relationship to Nature, humans or otherwise. In the perspective of intersubjective relations, one is now enveloped in the social role of a "proprietor," i.e., those who "have," contrasted to those who do not own properties, those who "have not." The social distancing look, both towards humans and Nature, is inaugurated by possession, just to turn those who possess into slaves of their possessions and hostages of the ideological mechanisms that aim at perpetuating their condition of proprietors. As to Nature, the unsuspected violence of appropriating part of Herself to one's juridic-political orbit, whilst at the same time denying other humans the same statute of proprietors and transforming these into paid workers, transforms one into a tool of Her destruction and a tool of the ideological segregation between those who "have and have not" explosive social stratification. By relegating the Other, natural and human, to the sphere of instrumental objectivity, we finally become "the tools of our tools."

Moreover, and here lies one of the big "knots" and ambivalences not only of Thoreau's thought but of the thinking about technique itself, as far as the instrumental use of technique itself is concerned. The interposition and mediation of an instrumental array of "things" (tools, instruments) between ourselves and Nature not only distances ourselves from Her, since we start identifying ourselves with our prolonged limbs, the tools originated in technique, but it is through technique itself that we can gather more knowledge about Nature and ourselves. The indispensability of technique, thus, transforms us, literally, into "tools of our tools" in more than one way. It is important to note here, I guess, that more than denouncing technique per se as the source of all our evils, or trying to depict Thoreau as a technophobe, the important aspect to be bore in mind is that, when we embark in a process of "thingification" of our true nature, our looks get so distorted in the process that we cannot even contemplate anymore, with clarity, the possibility of rethinking technique and, by implication, our nature and Nature Herself. We have thoroughly instrumentalized ourselves so much in the process, relegating our subjectivity to the sphere of objectivity in the process, that we tend to forget that the *homo faber*, "man, the maker," without the "*sapiens*" is not human anymore. From another viewpoint, it is technique itself that makes our sedentarism, physical and ideological, possible, through agriculture and architecture, as our titanic benefactor, Prometheus, never tires of reminding us. Technique domesticates us in more than one sense, and that process of domestication is integral to our deforming of the landscape, both internal and external ones.

Hence, the mastering of the techniques that make sedentism possible, architecture and agriculture among them, our apparent dominium over Nature necessarily implies the nefarious obverse of the coin: our domestication by becoming tools ourselves, in as much as our relationship with Nature becomes mediated by tools and techniques. Oblivious to that extraordinarily important fact humankind distance from Nature grows into such a chasm that we cannot contemplate anymore our irrevocable belonging to Her. Therefore, with the objectification and instrumentalization of our subjectivity, the progressive distancing and disconnection from our natural ontological belonging shaped by the unconscious inherited layers of domesticating ideological processes of possession, the unreflected usage of techniques and tools, are created the conditions of possibility to the taming of our wild, savage nature, obliterating the consciousness of our potential aesthetic—and ecstatic-symbiotic non-dual interdependence with Nature. That is the main reason why we need to emphasize Thoreau's thought as a "wild thought," what makes a poetic meditation on it an extraordinary opportunity not only to better understand the flourishing of civilizing processes and its convoluted problems, but to try to think out the implicit potentialities of a "Pedagogy of awakening," a reversal of our unfortunate estrangement from Nature, a pedagogy towards the possibility of another type of engagement with Nature, one that is based on the two-pronged cultivation of Nature and self-culture as well. *Colere*: cultivation, as the ancients used to say and, once again, a reminder of Emerson's *"Gnothi sauton* and study nature" programmatic invitation.

If Heraclitus was right, if it is true that "Nature loves to hide,"[54] one wonders where She might do so, given Her omnipresence, unless he means that by revealing Herself She hides Herself in Her revealing process, veiling the very mystery of the revelation itself. Yet, due to our alienation and peculiar forgetfulness of our natural ontological belonging, maybe an obvious place for Her to hide—and for us to start seeking—one that hitherto apparently has not attracted a lot of attention could be, as Thoreau so vehemently argued for, inside ourselves. It is tempting for me, thus, to read Heraclitus' aphorism as an optimum opportunity to embark on a hide and seek game with Nature having Thoreau as an extraordinary tracker, a faithful interpreter of Nature's hieroglyphs that, once decoded, might lead us towards the possibility of actualizing that ancient, venerable and beautiful project of "living according to Nature," with its promise of serenity as its result. Therefore, it seems incumbent on us to start that apophatic approach of cleaning and leveling the field for the ulterior construction of "loftier structures," as Henry says. Taking his thesis that we are Nature at prima facie value, the first and most important question immediately arises: "If we are really Nature, why do we forget our original natural condition?" Such a question, as I believe we all agree, is not only exceedingly ambitious, but may very well be unanswerable: how could one pretend to unravel the infinitely complex tapestry of causal necessity that stretches back infinitely and lies hidden and woven into such a question? More modestly, I believe that an attempt of describing the process of how we actually distance ourselves from Nature might help us to throw more light on the problem; thus, instead of asking for the why or the wherefore, let us try, in a propaedeutic manner, attempt to answer "How was it possible to forget our natural belonging" first and then, if our answer so allows, attempt a higher flight. However, to do so, we need to back, once again to the Promethean myth and hope that he might help us to escape the labyrinth we find ourselves in.

NOTES

1. Henry D. Thoreau *Translations*, Ed. K.P. Van Anglen, Princeton, Princeton University Press, 1986. It is unfortunate that there is not yet, to my knowledge, any monograph focusing on Thoreau's work as translator. His choice of works—and

words—might throw some light on some very important aspects of his work. Kevin Van Anglen's introduction to Thoreau's *Translations* volume of the Princeton edition of his works is an excellent starting point.

2. *Ibid.*

3. Thoreau, H. D. *Journal.* In: Witherell, E. H.; Howarth, W. L.; Sattelmeyer, R.; Blanding, T. (Eds.). *The Writings Of Henry D. Thoreau.* Princeton: Princeton University Press, 1981. V.I. *ournal*, vol. I, pp. 116–17; Thoreau, H. D. *Walden,* Princeton: Princeton University Press, 1971, p. 100.

4. Most of the scholarship on Thoreau addresses this issue with a plethora of diverging perspectives. I do believe the many tensions of this issue in Thoreau's works are insoluble, thanks to his "perspectvism," his attempt of looking at phenomena from plural perspectives, as we shall see later on.

5. Stoicism in particular, v. Epictetus and Marcus Aurelius.

6. The following observations are construed over the first pages of *Walden*.

7. *Walden*, p. 8.

8. *Idem*, p. 7.

9. *What offends me most in my compositions is the moral element in them. Journal*, vol. I, p. 316.

10. I shall return to that further on.

11. *Walden*, p. 5.

12. *Ibid*, pp. 5–7.

13. I believe Thoreau's relationship with Aristotle, *via* Greek writers like Theophrastus, and Latin ones like Pliny, Columella and others, deserves a more profound treatment, both in method, scope, vocabulary and goal.

14. Thoreau's experience as a teacher both in Concord's public school system as well as in a private school run by himself and his brother John ended, in the first case in exasperation and in the second in frustration.

15. As mentioned earlier, Thoreau is ambiguous about free-will and determinism, as we shall see further on. This may seem a moot point to some, however, if free-will is the basis of almost every single conceivable Ethics (Stoics and Spinoza's are among the very few exceptions), it is decisive to the claim that one is capable of reforming or changing one's practices, ways and beliefs.

16. *Walden*, p. 4.

17. I will return to that while commenting his understanding of Krsna's advice to Arjuna in the *Bhagavad-Gita*.

18. *Walden*, p. 5.

19. *Idem*, p. 6.

20. *Ibidem*, p. 8.

21. *Ibidem*, p. 8.

22. In Aristotle, there are four cases that help explaining the nature and scope of a being: the material cause, the formal, the efficient and the final one. The last is the *telos*, the rationale for the existence of some being, is the most important of the four causes. This vocabulary crept, via Thomism, into Christian catechisms.

23. The bulk of *Walden's* chapters, as many have already noted, are painted in contrasting colors: Reading x Sounds; Solitude x Visitors; The Bean-field x The village; The ponds x Baker farm; Higher Laws x Brute neighbors; Winter x Spring.

24. *Walden*, p. 16.
25. *Idem*, pp. 14–15.
26. *Ibidem*, p. 9.
27. Referring, symptomatically, to the dark ages, *Journal*, vol I. p. 90.
28. *Untimely meditations. Schopenhauer as an educator*.
29. *Walden*, p. 9.
30. The idea that society is sick and Nature healthy pervades his whole work. E.g. *Walden*, p. 8, 127.
31. *Walden*, p. 69.
32. *Civil Disobedience [Resistance to Civil Government]*, in Thoreau, H. D. *Collected Essays And Poems*. The Library Of America, Vol. 124. New York: The Library Of America, 2001. p. 205.
33. *Walking*, in Thoreau, H. D. *Collected Essays And Poems*. The Library Of America, Vol. 124. New York: The Library Of America, 2001, p. 225.
34. His most explicitly political essays, *Civil Disobedience, Herald of Freedom, Slavery in Massachusetts*, the Captain John Brown cycle, among others, tend to assume a much more urgent need of reformation than extinction of the State properly, immediate slavery abolition being the central interest of his writings. Thus, they touch lightly upon Political Philosophy properly, but it would be certainly extremely interesting to be able to hear what he might say about the necessary natural origins of the social institutions, unless, of course, he understands—and I don't think he ever came close to that—the State to be an *artificial* construction, what might clash with his primordial thesis that humans are part and parcel of Nature.
35. *A Week* p. 108–9
36. *A Week* p. 108–9
37. *Natural History of Massachusetts*, in Thoreau, H. D. *Collected Essays And Poems*. The Library Of America, Vol. 124. New York: The Library Of America, 2001, p. 22.
38. "The effect of a good government is to make life more valuable, of a bad one, to make it less valuable." *Slavery in Massachusetts*, in Thoreau, H. D. *Collected Essays And Poems*. The Library Of America, Vol. 124. New York: The Library Of America, 2001, p. 344.
39. More than a theoretically sustained reflection on the State, he seems more concerned with the need to "reform" government, thus, a reformist and not a revolutionary, a radical anarchist defending the end of the State *per se*.
40. *Walden*, p. 395
41. *Ibid.*, p. 346.
42. Greece, Rome, Britain and the US.
43. Maybe through his reading of Lucretius?
44. Did Thoreau read Epicure?
45. *Walden*, p. 332.
46. *Idem*, p. 333.
47. *Prometheus Bound*, l. 505. Aeschylus' version of the myth is one among many; there are many variations: Hesiod, Apollodorus, Plato, Ovid, Diodorus Siculus *et al*. This translation is by David Greene in *The complete Greek Tragedies*, vol. I,

Aeschylus. Edited and translated by David Greene and Richard Lattimore. Chicago: The University of Chicago Press, p. 329. The play has been the object of a plethora of different interpretations; here, we shall engage it focusing on Prometheus' role as a benevolent cultural hero whose gifts are a mixed blessing and the repercussions of the story for Thoreau.

48. Prometheus knew the name of Zeus' offspring who would eventually overthrow him, exactly like Zeus did to his father, Cronus. This is Prometheus' only trump and, according to fragments of Aeschylus' *Prometheus Unbound*, Zeus finally releases Prometheus after he reveals the woman Zeus is to avoid so that he won't beget the son who is supposed to overthrow him. In other sources Herakles frees Prometheus.

49. *Protagoras* 321a–322e *in* Plato. *Complete Works*. Edited By John M. Cooper. Indianapolis/Cambridge: Hackett Publishing Company, 1997.

50. *Prometheus bound*, ll. 440–60.

51. *Paradise (to be) regained. In* Thoreau, H. D. *Collected Essays And Poems*, p. 135. This passage comes from one of the most interesting and extraordinarily poorly read essays of Thoreau, "Paradise (to be) regained." There, Thoreau reflects about the nature of technique and its instrumentalization in order to go back to our pre-lapsarian state. It is a thorough comment on a book called *The paradise within the Reach of all Men, without Labor, by Powers of Nature and Machinery. An address to all intelligent Men. In two parts*. By J. A. Etzler. Part First. Second English Edition. pp. 55. London, 1842. Besides the quite fantastic title, a Thoreauvian *aporia* in itself, the essay throws an extremely fecund light on many of the points covered in our reflection. It begs further work on it. Thoreau's fascinating mythmaking on the railroad and the train in *Walden* is another of the many instances of his pendular relationship with technique.

52. Notwithstanding the anthropological and historical controversies that surround the events that ushered in the agricultural revolution in the region of the Crescent Fertile circa 8000 b.c.e., there is no doubt that the phenomenon of agriculture was central do the process of sedentism. Of course, that does not mark the end of nomadism *per se*, since even today some relatively small nomadic groups are found all over the globe. However, one cannot doubt that those historical events shaped the foundation of western civilization. Thoreau himself seems to be acutely aware of the issue, in as much as he tended to counterpoint Western sedentary political structures to non-Western ones, typically Native Americans nomadism.

53. *Journal*, vol. I, p. 368.

54. *Phúsis krúptesthai philein*. DK 123. *In* Freeman, Kathleen. *Ancilla to the Presocratic philosophers*. Cambridge, Mass: Harvard University Press, 1996, p. 33. This is one of the most commented fragments of Heraclitus and we are certainly not trying to propose any new line of interpretation here, but to utilize Heraclitus' aphorism as a point of departure to understand how and why we came to perceive ourselves as different and distant from the natural web.

Chapter 3

Sacramental Technique

There seems to be no way of reflecting about Nature without bringing to the fore Her generally perceived complementary other, Civilization/Culture. I say "generally perceived" because, as we have already seen, Thoreau was one of the very few thinkers who refused to accept such dichotomy and, in an early entry of his *Journal*, he takes the bull by the horns. Unsurprisingly, the register used is, as in the most decisive moments of his reflections, mythopoetic, and *Prometheus* is, once again, the psychopomp that leads the way through the labyrinthine meanders of this seminal and difficult issue:

"the mythologies, those vestiges of ancient poems, the world's inheritance, still reflecting some of the original hues . . . these are the materials and hints for a history of the rise and progress of the race. How from the condition of ants it arrived to the condition of men, how arts were invented gradually,—let a thousand surmises shed some light on this story . . . if we rise above this wisdom for the day, we shall expect that this morning of the race, in which they have been supplied with the simplest necessaries,—with corn and wine and honey and oil and fire and articulate speech and agricultural and other arts,—reared up by degrees from the condition of ants to men, will be succeeded by a day of equally progressive splendor; that, in the lapse of divine periods, other divine agents and godlike men will assist to elevate the race as much above its present condition."[1]

Some preliminaries are relevant here: (i) Mythology is, in a certain way, history for Thoreau;[2] (ii) *Prometheus bound* is the script of the narrative;[3] (iii) There is progress in history, and it is or can be brought about by cultural heroes like Prometheus; (iv) the scheme shows a progressive complexification of arts and techniques with an implicit looming concomitant decadence, from the basic necessities towards luxury; (v) techniques raise humans from the level of animals. However, radically more important than all this, is this one single fact, that illuminates the whole of Thoreau's thinking: (vi) myth is the language that Nature, or Reality or Being utilizes to sing Her infinite song of truth and beauty. It is Nature Herself, through every singular being, that reveals Herself in Her myriad individual songs. That symphony of voices that irrupts as life, as a cyclic reality of sublimity, horror, joy, pain, that set of endless songs played by the "Aeolian harps," as Thoreau names it, is reflected in the kaleidoscopic fractals of beauty and truth that percolate throughout Nature, enlivening and vascularizing Her, literally, cosmically, in the sense of harmony and order seen above. Even if we sometimes can only hear the cacophony, that is only because we are not able to tune ourselves in the proper key. It is not a coincidence that the ultimate non-dual experience of merging with Nature for Henry is described in musical terms. It is not a coincidence, either, that Pythagoras and the "harmony of the spheres" is invoked as a testimony to the process, as we shall see further on. Myth is the most archaic linguistic embodiment of Nature in humans, its most singular, beautiful and true voice. It is the language used by reality itself to tell its history, from the most primeval moment until now and stretching into an unending horizon. Moreover, according to Henry's words, myth is the language used in the "morning of the race," apparently indicating, again by using his Greece-morning-youth-Spring grid, the ancestral link between myth and the experience of beginnings and belongings, both diachronically, i.e., as the most archaic register of the experience of human beings from the primeval times, as well as synchronically, that is, in the radical nature of its pervasiveness right now, meaning that, at this moment, that very same experience of belonging is available to all those who open themselves up and converge to the horizon of that possibility, engaging themselves in that anamnetic and genealogical effort. In this sense, Thoreau would certainly subscribe to the thesis that "in the beginning was the Word," since myth as the narratological dimension of Being is the ablest correlate to the radicular pervasiveness of beauty and truth within the cosmos. Nature speaks, sings continuously Her history and Her attempts at self-discovery through Her infinite singular manifestations and modes of being and processes, and the hero-poets are the human mediums that She utilizes as flutes of Her infinite variations and modulations. To become a flute on Her lips and being able to decipher her material hieroglyphic imprints in the natural and material world seem to be Thoreau's mission on this earth. The felicity of Nature's choice is unquestionable. Yet, we have only arrived at the beginning of the thread that might walk us out of the maze of our reflection on technique. Now we must try to unravel it and, with luck, be able to leave this labyrinth, even if it is not possible to leave holding the trophy of truth after of our encounter with the Minotaur of technique, at least alive, to tell other of the perils that lie ahead.

"Every art of humankind comes from Prometheus."⁴ The word translated here as "art" in the original Greek is *"téchnai,"* the nominative plural of *"téchne."* Aeschylus uses a word that has a very specific semantic range: art, technique, skill; a word whose destiny was to be inextricably connected to every reflection on culture, civilization and Nature. Contemporary Philosophy has dedicated a lot of attention to it, famously, Martin Heidegger in his many essays, *The Question Concerning Technology* especially.⁵ Respectfully distancing ourselves from the Black Forest saunterer, I aim at understanding here Technique as a distancing process, emphasizing its instrumental role in the dynamics of taming and obfuscating our original natural belonging, utilizing, for such project, the problematization of two experiences to which Thoreau has dedicated a lot of attention: the construction of his hut and the tilling of his bean-field; I will take both experiences as two exemplary activities that were instrumental in fabricating the shroud of oblivion we wear concerning our natural standing, then, later on, I will try to explore in which ways Thoreau offers us a set of practices that might lift the veil from the alienating condition that stems from that obliviousness.

The path we shall thread towards our poetic meditation shall be a reflection on the phenomenological materialization of building and tilling. By phenomenological materialization I shall understand a return to the aesthetical possibilities that lie in the processes of building and tilling, meaning, in fact, to build a hut and till a field, in other words, a return to things and processes. Thoreau, artisan of word and wood, meditated much on the hidden meanings of carving a home out of Nature and tilling the earth, thus, as an artist of thought and matter, I shall invoke, on his behalf, Socrates' testimony who, famously, thought that artisans were the first to be consulted concerning the nature of the many *téchnai*;⁶ according to him, contrary to poets and politicians, artisans do know something, the problem with technicians being, as with other specialists, they extrapolate their limited knowledge and, like everyone else, assume to have a knowledge they in fact do not possess. Therefore, let us Socratically limit, at this juncture, Thoreau's reflections to the perimeter of seeding homes and beans, since there is no reason to doubt Thoreau when he boasts "I speak understandingly on this subject[i.e., building], for I have made myself acquainted with it both theoretically and practically"⁷ Therefore, in a Socratic/Thoreauvian fashion, we shall first ask Thoreau, the technician, about the nature of building/architecture and tilling/agriculture, postponing our philosophical quest for the time being and, proceeding methodically in our attempt of understanding the constitutive elements of those experiences so that, later on, we may depict in the clearest possible way the topography of the philosophical landscape that emerges from those practical endeavors. Taking *téchne* as our clue, it is time to start our investigation on those two processes: first, building—or, as Thoreau calls it, architecture; then, we shall proceed to tilling or, as he calls it, agriculture. As philologists say, when in doubt as to where to start from, ask the word.

Architecture, the "most important technique" or "oldest technique" may be decomposed into *archi / arche*, which can mean either "importance, centrality, superiority" (as in "archrival, archduke") or "origin, past, old age" (as in "archeology" or "archaic" / "arcane"). *Téchne*, as we have already seen, means "art, skill, technique" and it clearly points to the production or an instrument, a method, to make/produce something. It is attested in many ancient languages (Sanskrit *takṣati*, Latin *tego*[8]) and it is a central topic in *Walden*. Whether etymology is a good hermeneutic tool as Thoreau seems to believe, since the more ancient a word is the closer to the capacity of describing precisely reality—like the mythic register—, the fundamental shade of meaning that emerges from the expression "architecture," seems to point to its role as an *Urtechnik*, "a primordial technique," both in terms of antiquity as well as importance.

> "We may imagine a time when, in the infancy of the human race, some enterprising mortal crept into a hollow in a rock for shelter. Every child begins the world again, to some extent, and loves to stay out doors, even in wet and cold. It plays house, as well as horse, having an instinct for it. Who does not remember the interest with which when young he looked at shelving rocks, or any approach to a cave? It was the natural yearning of that portion of our most primitive ancestor which still survived in us. From the cave we have advanced to roofs of palm leaves, of bark and boughs, of linen woven and stretched, of grass and straw, of boards and shingles, of stones and tiles. At last, we know not what it is to live in the open air, and our lives are domestic in more senses than we think. From the hearth to the field is a great distance."[9]

As it is typical of Thoreau whenever he starts an analysis of any phenomenon,[10] he first embarks on a genealogical essay to trace the trajectory of the phenomenon from its incipience until its hodiernal state, be it the origin of forests from the dispersion of seeds, apple matrixes, clothing, shelter or food, a thorough bibliographical review being a premium of his methodological approach. The genesis, the arche is always the springboard from where he plunges into the sea of things and processes, exemplarily in the first part of *Walden*, when he meditates on the necessaries of life, that genealogical-etymological dynamic introduces us to brief historical and axiological presentations of clothing, shelter, food and heating, if the alert reader recalls, the building blocks for the already mentioned project of "living according to Nature" or, in other words, for the "Pedagogy of awakening." When I say historical and axiological, I mean them in the sense of that already observed ingrained Thoreauvian equation: from original pristine simplicity/efficiency/purity to its deformation into complication/encumbrance/luxury. One might multiply the instances of such contrasts both as a methodological as well as a rhetoric device, "civilization" / "savages," to the detriment of the first, being also a favorite one.[11]

As to shelter, one of the "necessaries" contemplated by architecture, Thoreau goes all the way back to Adam and Eve—always the inescapable mythological pre-lapsarian datum to start with—and thence to the supposed evolutionary scheme: caves, roofs of palm leaves, woods, stones and tiles.[12] In this specific instance, he seems to believe that in order to fully comprehend and answer the question "what is a house?,"[13] its real end and finality, one has to make a historical and axiological digression to understand the subtle nuances of the issue at hand, instantiated, in this particular case, in the art of building. He never forgets that the end, the finality of something is the most important question to be asked about it, be it a house, food or life.[14] In the case of a house it is to warm and protect us. Again, it seems implicit in his arguments our epistemic malfunction for, if my reading is correct, he does not appear to doubt that once one is shown the best option (a simple house), one is certainly bound to opt for it instead of the worst one (the luxurious), and his many historical, economic, social, political and spiritual arguments can be better understood as binding unfoldings of that genealogical and axiological axiomatic equation. He goes on in some detail about the contrasts:

"The very simplicity and nakedness of man's life in the primitive ages imply this advantage at least, that they left him still but a sojourner in nature. When he was refreshed with food and sleep he contemplated his journey again. He dwelt, as it were, in a tent in this world, and was either threading the valleys, or crossing the plains, or climbing the mountain tops. But lo! men have become the tools of their tools. The man who independently plucked the fruits when he was hungry is become a farmer; and he who stood under a tree for shelter, a housekeeper. We now no longer camp as for a night, but have settled down on earth and forgotten heaven. We have adopted Christianity merely as an improved method of agri-culture. We have built for this world a family mansion, and for the next a family tomb."[15]

The first thing that seems to emerge from such a rich text is its ambiguity. We have seen above that there is progress in History, effected by those cultural heroes like Prometheus. Here, the signal inverts: History seems to be a continuous decadence from its springs on. Simplicity and nomadism seem to translate, symbolically, the possibility of a harmonious intimacy with Nature; Technique and sedentism, as manifested by agriculture and architecture—fall, alienation. This passage is symptomatic of Thoreau's most fundamental axioms and can be seen as a nutshell of this chapter. Indeed, at this point, he seems to share with some ancient authors the belief that there is no actual progress in History at all, on the contrary, like some Greek and Latin mythographers[16] who hold that humankind falls continuously from a pristine archaic vigor that is incomparably closer to the true source of life and Being into a debased state of corruption and unhappiness. The closer one is to Nature, the more archaic the phenomenon, the happier the subject and less corrupted the state. However, faithful to our program, it is high time to turn to architecture and its problematic obverse, sedentism.

The first thing it seems relevant to notice about architecture as technique, as a *tool*, is its attempt to overcome the natural condition of shelter as a primeval *refuge*, so, to deliberately carve out of Nature according to a plan, to a *"project"* (literally, a "throwing-forth"), implies an intentional effort towards the consecration of a dwelling that, whilst constituted spatially inside and materially from Nature, is subjectively perceived and becomes in reality outside and different from Nature. This phenomenon is, I believe, an important key to understanding one of the most important dynamics for our distancing and subsequent alienation from Nature. That "occupation" pro-ject, literally, the drive for the "occupation" of Nature, the casting forward together of necessity and intentionality happens first in imagination, that singular instance where abstraction marries reality in its incipient will to transform and possess the perceived passive Other, Nature, an "Other" in which our ancestors seemed uncomfortable to blend in anymore. That differentiation happened, I imagine, because of an estrangement of our enlightened primitive late primate forefathers who, now aware of their singularity (thought, language and tools) could not recognize themselves anymore in the mirror of the Other, the rest of natural beings. Thus, what was a once a refuge became, through the mastering of some tools/techniques, a process of violent domestication of Nature. That perceived difference, originated from introspection and observation of Nature, encapsulated in our self-segregation from the rest of creatures may, in that light, have been the first sign of anthropocentric hierarchical polarization with the natural Other as well, so that what was first a refuge slowly turned into a project of occupation, demarcation and allocation of the natural space. Fear becomes knowledge, then domination, *dominium*: the immediate results from the beginning of the adventure of "*Gnothi sauton* and study Nature" start: internally, introspection; externally, the occupation and deformation of the original landscape.

So that now instead of a cave we had a *domus*, a house. And from *domus* came *dominium*, "lording upon," "domination," the allocation of what was common to what is now demarcated; from dominium, firstly *de facto* and much later *de jure*, comes *dominus*, the Lord, the owner. Those who were once squatters became Lords, owners. That is also the probable reason that explains why habitat, "the place one lives," comes from Latin *habere*, "to possess." An inhabitant is one who occupies or possesses a certain spot of transformed Nature. Unfortunately, with domus, dominium and dominus, domestication appears, someone or something "dominated," "under the dominium of something or someone." The idea seems pretty clear by now: our dominium of Nature implies a dialectical tension between those who dominate and those who are dominated; those dominated are not only the ones who are in any way subjugated in a hierarchical polarization, be it animal, humans or Nature in general, rather, the first ideological "victim" of the process of dominium/domestication, is the subject herself of dominium who, unconsciously, also becomes domesticated in the process, necessarily falling under the weight of the dominium one now possesses: bound to the possession comes the oblivious self-dispossession of our natural belonging. What was subject becomes object and what was object, becomes subject, and the inversion of roles point to the crushing load of possession. Karl Marx could not come up with a better example of alienation and would certainly agree with these words: "I see young men, my townsmen, whose misfortune it is to have inherited farms, houses, barns, cattle, and farming tools . . . how many a poor immortal soul have I met well nigh crushed and smothered under its load, creeping down the road of life."[17] Farms, houses, barns, tools: who is the subject and what is the object now? Or, as Thoreau describes the process: "from staying under a tree to housekeepers." The internal and external distances went through are enormous. Debts and mortgages are soon to follow. Yet, and this is decisive, even such a prolonged process of denaturalization could not completely hide the veiled content of the original, archaic movement of distancing. It is not for nothing that Thoreau is confident in saying "the house is still but a sort of porch at the entrance of a burrow"[18] Now, that, as we have already seem, is a very pregnant statement for many reasons. The many layers interposed between our demarcated space and Nature still betrays the original finality of shelter as refuge, even with our debasing and transformation of Nature. As he sees it: "almost all man's improvements, so called, as the building of houses, and cutting down of the forest and all large trees, simply deforms the landscape, make it more tame and cheap."[19] Even long after the occupation and transformation of Nature, Her taming, nonetheless, a house is still a "burrow," and that is a very interesting choice of word, as we have already seen. Taming, deformation, distance, possession: the vocabulary of the continuous falsification of our nature, Nature's nature and our belonging inextricably to Her. Those concepts form the perilous equation that determines the veiling of our savage, original face and helps creating a travesty of humanity, that henceforth shall be doomed to possessing Nature, and not being one with Her anymore. As to building itself, however, the technique that makes that possession possible, and once again, ambiguously, Thoreau has some nice words to commend it:

> "It would be worth the while to build still more deliberately than I did, considering, for instance, what foundation a door, a window, a cellar, a garret, have in the nature of man, and perchance never raising any superstructure until we found a better reason for architecture it than our temporal necessities even. There is some of the same fitness in a man's building his own house that there is in a bird's building its own nest. Who knows but if men constructed their dwellings with their own hands, and provided food for themselves and families simply and honestly enough, the poetic faculty would be universally developed, as birds universally sing when they are so engaged? But alas! we do like cowbirds and cuckoos, which lay their eggs in nests which other birds have built, and cheer no traveller with their chattering and unmusical notes. Shall we forever resign the pleasure of construction to the carpenter? What does architecture amount to in the experience of the mass of men? I never in all my walks came across a man engaged in so simple and natural an occupation as building his house."[20]

This reflection on building and dwelling seems to be, literally, a/the cornerstone of Thoreau's meditation on a very specific and beloved technique of his: building. We are building (and tilling) animals. Builders and tillers. Technical beings, in other words. Deliberation, that is, care, tenderness and awareness in building—as in tilling—as we shall soon see, articulates many ideas for Henry: the belonging to a burrow built by oneself, the correspondence between the internal and the external realities—a sacramental relationship—, the experience of building a house and shaping oneself concomitantly. So many fascinating ideas irrupt from that single meditation. Ideally, as per the next quote, a dweller should or could be a builder, so that one might be able to be aware of the multiple convergenges of meaning inaugurated by those technical experiments. On the contrary, by renouncing the pleasures of architecture/building and agriculture, relegating it to professionals, we miss much more than simply the action of construction itself: (i) we lose touch with our burrow, our most archaic belonging, deeply nestled in Nature; (ii) we miss the pleasure and knowledge that emerges from reflecting and experiencing the many deeply entwined processes involved in "building" and, worst of all (iii) we interpose other humans and their tools between us, our burrow and Nature Herself. The estrangement and distance from Nature grows and grows. In this perspective, when one is responsible for building one's own home, there is always the possibility, by handling materials like wood, earth and metals—Thoreau was obsessed with listing all the materials he used in his building at Walden—that a deeper connection might emerge from the elements involved in "architecture": soil—materials—inhabitant. It seems that for Thoreau, the continuum of location, the allocation of materials, the planning and transformation, the sweating, the pains and joys, as well as reflecting about everything that concerns the construction, that is, meditating upon all the elements that wraps everything together under the act of building, might minimize the violence of possession and the deformation of the landscape. Strangely, for him, the building of one's home *naturalizes* and *diminishes* the violence of Nature's appropriation by us and the artifice of building itself, by literally making it both a *poiesis* and a *praxis*, two important words derived from the Greek verbs (*poiein/poieō* and *prattein/prāssō*), utilized, in Greek, for "doing," "producing" something. The philosophical pedigree of those concepts is ancient, and the richness that unfolds from exploring those verbs is worth considering here. Let us take Aristotle as our guide, aware that what he wrote about those terms might fill volumes, and that I shall certainly dilute and flatten the richness of his meditation on those issues, my intention being, here, to indicate how those concepts might help us in exploring Thoreau's perspectives on "producing" and "belonging" in relation to that that is being produced, be it a house or crops. In other words, I want to inquiry at this point how those two terms might relate to Thoreau's reflection on technique and in which manner Thoreau articulates his thought within the framework of reorienting our relationship with technology in general, trying to understanding the possibility of prolonging oneself in one's productions, a "sacramental relationship," so that technique might be not only understood as distancing, but as a condition of possibility to revealing something about either ourselves or Nature, in other words, to transform technique into a tool of revelation, of transformation, of self-knowledge, instead of a tool of alienation.

Asking his forgiveness for debasing his precious reflections, according to Aristotle, who devoted a lot of attention to both concepts (*praxis, poiesis*) in his ethical writings, especially in the *Politics* and the *Nichomacean Ethics*, praxis has to do with every action that is an end in itself, or whose product is not different from the producer: political activity and the discourse being two exemplary instantiations of it, and the ones I shall be exploring. Poiesis, on the other hand, is the making of something that produces something different from the producer: a house, a jug.[21] The arguments in Aristotle are further complicated by the idea of finality, which we may skip for the time being, since what I am trying to point out to, here, in the context of Thoreau's activities of building and tilling, is that in terms of praxis, his building of his hut might be read in different perspectives. As a political statement (praxis), it can be read as: (i) a refusal of the progressive specialization of productive activities in society; (ii) as a signpost of political autarky and distancing from the *polis*, from the community; (iii) as a discourse, building/tilling/writing—very approximated experiences for Thoreau—can be seen as very useful instruments of self-discovery, self-construction and self-polishing, as we shall soon see, since Thoreau defends the thesis that every external building should, ideally, correspond to an internal reality, in a sacramental bond:

"What of architectural beauty I now see, I know has gradually grown from within outward, out of the necessities and character of the indweller, who is the only builder,—out of some unconscious truthfulness, and nobleness, without ever a thought for the appearance; and whatever additional beauty of this kind is destined to be produced will be preceded by a like unconscious beauty of life."[22]

The relationship internal-external is further reinforced and deepened by the possibility of understanding it in a sacramental way: "I have scarcely heard of a truer sacrament, that is, as the dictionary defines it, 'outward and visible sign of an inward and spiritual grace.'"[23] Although this passage comes from a reflection on furniture, it may be amplified, as we shall soon see, to the other instances (building, tilling, even walking into a wood), where that sacramental relationship becomes a patina that envelops with beauty and truth an external phenomenon, especially a technical one, which, in a sort of way, legitimizes and sacralises its use, as in the case of building and tilling.

Such convergence of finalities (the exterior/interior sacramental dynamic) group art/technique, knowledge/wisdom and beauty/awakening: in his vocabulary, they develop our "poetic faculty." And poetry is certainly a very apt word to describe with precision the many shades of meaning intended. If "poiein," this "poetical building" is to be adopted as a preferred reading, then, a poetically built dwelling, the ultimate type of Architecture envisaged by Thoreau, is literally cemented with poetry, and the performance of building might turn the act of building into a poetical point of convergence between builder, building and Nature, triggering the transformation of technique into a tool of self-transformation and self-revelation. If we humans are, as Thoreau seems to believe, building beings, constructors, when one neglects that potential source of "poetical" occupation, a poetical building of one's burrow, one might probably be renouncing the possibility of a poetical dwelling. As building animals, technical beings, we dwell poetising (*poiesis*) and practising (*praxis*) things-doing, producing stuff—there is no escaping it. Thus, by building, by poetising a house, one's own house, one would ideally transform Nature poetically, carefully, tenderly as well, without deforming one's nature, technique's nature and Nature Herself so dramatically.

Yet, as it turns out, as it ordinarily happens, without any sort of poetry and sacredness by just buying and not building one's own home, one is now the proud owner of a house, but, with his characteristic humorous *schadenfreude* and ironic twist, when Thoreau rhetorically asks: "what is a house," the answer is "a *sedes*, a seat."[24] That is an extraordinarily important statement for a couple of reasons. On the one hand, there is a profound semantic tension that underlies the Latin expression *sedes*. It means (i) chair, (ii) home, residence, (iii) seat and (iv) settlement, habitation. Also, there is a shade of sacredness in the expression, as in *Sancta sedes*, "The Holy See," the Vatican, as the "seat" of Catholic Christendom, just like every cathedral (related to "chair" as well) is the "seat" of every bishop. Thus, the expression relates a house to a sacred place. On the other hand, a house/sedes is the place where one sits, where one settles, where sedentism, the sedating form of sedentarism begins to occur: sedes, seat, sela, settle, saddle, sedative, sediment, settlement, all of them are derived from the Latin verb *sidere*, to sit. Again, the choice of word could not be more precise, pregnant and revealing. Thoreau's sensibility and musical ear for words is really astounding; to sit is to stop: change is over, movement is over and sauntering is over. The sap of life stops flowing. Even if one possesses a "country seat," the best sort of a house according to Thoreau, it nonetheless spells a danger of self-confinement and domestication. Of course, it is possible—and Thoreau thought it should probably be mandatory—that we do not forsake the pleasure of architecture: we all should try our hands at building our own places, more ideally still, to build in a "deliberate way," that is, making the external house a reflection of an interior building, or rebuilding of the Self and, as we have just seen, he also wonders if in the process of building our houses ourselves we might not develop our "poetic faculty."[25] However, it would be an exercise in futility to quote the scores of instances where he contrasts change, movement, walking and renewal with their appalling contraries: domestication, taming, cocooning, sclerosis.[26] For someone who believed that a day without walking, without sauntering was a lost day, who believed that continuous renewal is a prerequisite to a higher life, as when serpents shed their skins in Springtime, the season of renovation, for whom Native Americans perennial nomadic lifestyle is particularly appealing and praised as something to be emulated, if not materially, at least intellectually and spiritually, the idea of loss of movement could be tragic. Moreover, epistemological nomadism or perspectivism, as I shall try to argue later on, sits at the very heart of Thoreau's epistemological approach to *Philosophia Naturalis*. Yet, architecture or building is not the only technique that was instrumental in domesticating both Nature and us. There is another sort of taming of Nature that concurs with the taming of our nature and with the deformation of Nature, and that is trough tilling, the cultivation of the fields, the culture of the *ager*, what we call agriculture, and it is time to turn to it now.

> "The village is the place to which the roads tend . . . the word is from the Latin villa, which, together with via, a way, or more anciently ved and vella, Varro derives from veho, to carry, because the villa is the place to and from which things are carried . . . hence, too apparently, the Latin word villis and our vile; also villain. This suggests what kind of degeneracy villagers are liable to."[27]

Again, for Thoreau, there is no talking of something without, first, contextualizing it in a more interdependent and relational way. To reflect on the wilderness, and the cultivated fields, it is necessary to locate them in a broader landscape. Thus, to interpret the role of the fields, the *ager*, it is unavoidable to talk about where they are located, and that is spread between the village and the forest.

> "Mediaeval, or law, Latin seems to have invented the word 'forest,' not being satisfied with silva, nemus, etc. Webster makes it from the same root with 'L.[atin]foris, Fr.[ench]hors, and the Saxon faran, to go, to depart.' The allied words 'all express distance from cities and civilization, and are from roots expressing departure or wandering,'—as if this newer term were needed to describe those strange, wild woods furthest from the centres of civilization."[28]

I guess the first thing due here is to characterize the fields, the ager, as the border, as a limit between the village and the forest. Thoreau did not like villages in general and most of the time his characterization of them are negative, as the *villain* wry comment shows. That is the probable rationale why *Walden*'s chapter "*The Village*" is the shortest of all chapters of the book, and also the reason why it lies squeezed between "*The Bean-Field*" and "*The Ponds*" chapters, Thoreau seeming to be in a hurry to describe his culture of beans, his working field of which he is so proud of and go sauntering by and swimming in the ponds. Interestingly, Thoreau has absolutely nothing positive to say about the village, not even caring to give us its name, Concord, its negative aspects being depicted in exactly two pages, the other pages of the tiny chapter recounting either his adventures going back in pitch black nights to his hut at *Walden* or gleefully reminiscing about his arrest. The village is a dangerous place[29] and one is safer in the woods in a pitch-black night, he seems to suggest.

As to Thoreau's genealogy of husbandry/agriculture, it follows exactly the same pattern of his analysis of architecture, both in its genealogical methodology as well as in its decadent and degrading trajectory: a mythological account that relates how from the purity of its pristine finality it was historically and culturally debased by a corrupt society:

> "Ancient poetry and mythology suggest, at least, that husbandry was once a sacred art; but it is pursued with irreverent haste and heedlessness by us, our object being to have large farms and large crops merely. We have no festival, nor procession, nor ceremony, not excepting our Cattle—shows and so—called Thanksgivings, by which the farmer expresses a sense of the sacredness of his calling, or is reminded of its sacred origin. It is the premium and the feast which tempt him. He sacrifices not to Ceres and the Terrestrial Jove, but to the infernal Plutus rather. By avarice and selfishness, and a grovelling habit, from which none of us is free, of regarding the soil as property, or the means of acquiring

property chiefly, the landscape is deformed, husbandry is degraded with us, and the farmer leads the meanest of lives. He knows Nature but as a robber. Cato says that the profits of agriculture are particularly pious or just, (*maximeque pius quæstus,*) and according to Varro the old Romans 'called the same earth Mother and Ceres, and thought that they who cultivated it led a pious and useful life, and that they alone were left of the race of King Saturn.'"[30]

It is relevant here to stress, once again, that human action, both in building and in agriculture, deform the landscape; again, the choice of words is precise. We transform the landscape while making it deteriorate through violence. The deformation of the landscape seems to mirror the corruption of our spirit since Nature, husbandry and we ourselves are all deformed in the same process by the logic of dominium and, later on, profit. The process of domestication, therefore, implies concurrent processes of multiple deformations where the feeling of possession of a slot of earth corrupts a once sacred relationship. The logic of profit replaces the bond of sacredness to the Earth and debases the farmer to the minuscule dimension of a robber. The appropriation of a slot of Nature corrupts not only our relationship to Earth, but the feeling of proprietariness towards Her legitimizes the use of violence against all those who occupy the coveted and potentially lucrative piece of land: flora, fauna, minerals and native populations. Very different was the attitude of the ancients. They revered the vascularization of the sacred in Nature, transforming Her into a temple, Herself worthy of worship:

> "I would that our farmers when they cut down a forest felt some of that awe which the old Romans did when they came to thin, or let in the light to, a consecrated grove, (lucum conlucare,) that is, would believe that it is sacred to some god. The Roman made an expiatory offering, and prayed, Whatever god or goddess thou art to whom this grove is sacred, be propitious to me, my family, and children, &c."[31]

What once was sacred became "resource," in a world that relegates even humanity to the level of "human resource," depriving its intrinsic worth and transforming it in just another factor of the capitalist mode of production. What once was the sacred playground of Pan and the nymphs became a waste land, an immemorial adversary that must be subjugated by iron and fire, clearing the sacred groves where teophanies and epiphanies were once possible in exchange of a plot of earth to be bought and sold: sacred estate became real estate. "As for a habitat, if I were not permitted still to squat, I might purchase one acre at the same price for which the land I cultivated was sold—namely, eight dollars and eight cents. But as it was, I considered that I enhanced the value of the land by squatting on it."[32]

The misguided perception of dominium leads both to the subjugation of the Other and to alienation from oneself; unfortunately, History, as we all know only too well, is abundantly clear about that. That seems to be the rationale behind Thoreau's celebration of his and his brother's non-ownership of land even after seeing the beauty and sacredness of the works of the farmer: "how fortunate were we who did not own an acre of those shores, who had not renounced our title to the Whole. One who knew how to appropriate the true value of this world would be the poorest man in it. The poor rich man! All he has is what he has bought."[33] The idea of non-ownership is revealing. As an extraordinary student of Earth, Her fauna, flora, rivers and myriad other forms, Thoreau once again throws light on the importance of finality. It is not the means that determine the end, but the other way round. Non-acquisitiveness conforms to Nature, proprietariness deforms Her. The impact of architecture, agriculture and other techniques go well beyond transformation; when one is bound to depict it as a deformation, as Thoreau does, it means that one cannot recognize anymore one's original condition. When one transforms one changes the form, when one deforms, one spoils the form, the original form or *eidos*, to use Platonic and Aristotelic vocabulary. When we transform something we just give it a different form, where the original substance can still be perceived; when we deform something we rob it of its identity, the original substance now being beyond recognition. That is exactly what we have caused to Nature and to ourselves. We have not only changed Nature or our own forms, we have spoilt, corrupted and destroyed, we have deformed them.

We cannot recognize ourselves anymore in our original form as natural beings, we have superimposed so many ideological and technological taming layers and processes between us and Her, we have receded so much from our natural belonging, that we have become a disembodied simulacrum of ideological, political and economic drives. To halt this most unfortunate alienating process, one has to take extreme measures, and Thoreau's sharp critique, his attempt at cauterization of that simulacrum certainly feels intolerably painful most of the time; however, one has to remember the finality of the project of cauterization: the halting of the process of the spread of the infection; then, if the apophatic process of cleansing, of dressing of the wound comes to a good term, it is time to apply the medicine, the "Pedagogy of awakening," so that the optimum result occurs: the promise of *eudaimonia*. It is this promise of wellness that sustains the unmitigated critique of our values and practices. After all, one has to keep in mind the good news, for according to Thoreau it is possible to change that sorry state of affairs through a deliberate effort of the will: "by a conscious effort of the mind we may stay aloof from actions and consequences."[34] Thus, according to him, it is possible to regain our natural condition by a voluntary option for new values and practices. Some of these values and practices which we shall see further on. As to technique and technology, one of the practices that Thoreau uses to mediate his relations with them, is to mythologize their products, be it architecture, agriculture or, interestingly, that new advent that heralded a new era: the railway and its locomotive, the train:

> "The whistle of the locomotive penetrates my woods summer and winter, sounding like the scream of a hawk sailing over some farmer's yard, informing me that many restless city merchants are arriving within the circle of the town, or adventurous country traders from the other side. As they come under one horizon, they shout their warning to get off the track to the other, heard sometimes through the circles of two towns. Here come your groceries, country; your rations, countrymen! Nor is there any man so independent on his farm that he can say them nay. And here's your pay for them! screams the countryman's whistle; timber like long battering rams going twenty miles an hour against the city's walls, and chairs enough to seat all the weary and heavy laden that dwell within them. With such huge and lumbering civility the country hands a chair to the city. All the Indian huckleberry hills are stripped, all the cranberry meadows are raked into the city. Up comes the cotton, down goes the woven cloth; up comes the silk, down goes the woollen; up come the books, but down goes the wit that writes them."[35]

The irony is multivalent, but the possibility of approaching, understanding and accepting the novelty comes, once more, from mythology:

> "When I meet the engine with its train of cars moving off with planetary motion,—or, rather, like a comet, for the beholder knows not if with that velocity and with that direction it will ever revisit this system, since its orbit does not look like a returning curve,—with its steam cloud like a banner streaming behind in golden and silver wreaths, like many a downy cloud which I have seen, high in the heavens, unfolding its masses to the light,—as if this travelling demigod, this cloud-compeller, would ere long take the sunset sky for the livery of his train; when I hear the iron horse make the hills echo with his snort like thunder, shaking the earth with his feet, and breathing fire and smoke from his nostrils, (what kind of winged horse or fiery dragon they will put into the new Mythology I don't know,) it seems as if the earth had got a race now worthy to inhabit it. If all were as it seems, and men made the elements their servants for noble ends! If the cloud that hangs over the engine were the perspiration of heroic deeds, or as beneficent to men as that which floats over the farmer's fields, then the elements and Nature herself would cheerfully accompany men on their errands and be their escort."[36]

Yet, the vigorous density and ultimate rationale of Thoreau's mythologizing of technology should not blind us to its continuous falsification of reality, its capacity of deforming Nature and the consequent oblivion of our most archaic belonging. Mythology, in this sense, can be understood as a heuristic and even hermeneutical mechanism to interpret and legitimize the usage of the whole gamut of the techniques, be it architecture in Aeschylus' Prometheus or the Fitchburg Railways in the contemporary newspapers. However, we must emphasize, here, that every technique (letters, building, tilling) was, originally, divine and sacred, as the myth tells us, and it was Prometheus that robbed them from their divine custodians, Athena and Hephaistos. It is important to expand on this sacred origin of the arts and crafts, since humans seem to have corrupted those divine powers that were given to us, and, moreover, we must remember that it were those very same sacred techniques that founded human civilization. In this sense, civilization is inaugurated by an act of violence (the robbery of the fire / techniques) that founds our culture. Once again, according to the myth, we have corrupted something that originally was sacred and divine, debasing them with our hybris.

However, one may ask: are we not so corrupted that it would be extremely hard to detect our true nature? Isn't the mirror of our consciousness so smudged and blurred by the many layers of civilization and culture that it would be virtually impossible to recognize our true, natural face? Isn't the process of alienation so profound as to render our anamnetic process ineffective? How can one recognize one's own natural form if one has no recollection of it anymore? Moreover—and by far the worst question of all: what is our true Nature? But to answer that terrible question, about our particular nature, we have to tackle an even worse one that has been looming around us for some time: "What is Nature?" And that is precisely our next challenge.

NOTES

1. Thoreau, H. D. *Journal*. In: Witherell, E. H.; Howarth, W. L.; Sattelmeyer, R.; Blanding, T. (Eds.). *The Writings Of Henry D. Thoreau*. Princeton: Princeton University Press, 1981. V.I., pp. 393–94.

2. As we shall see later on, this is one among many others instances of the impact of German idealism, especially Herder, Schlegel, Hölderlin and Schelling through Coleridge and others on Transcendentalism and Thoreau in particular.

3. *Prometheus bound*, ll. 447–506.

4. *Op. Cit.*

5. *Die frage nach der Technik*, an essay of his collection *Vorträge und Aufsätze* from 1954.

6. Cf. Plato's *Apology of Socrates*. It is a controversial problem throughout the History of Philosophy, especially in contemporary Continental Philosophy, as to who is more capable to understand the nature of technique.

7. Thoreau, H. D. *Walden*, Princeton: Princeton University Press, 1971, p. 40.

8. The Latin verb *tego* means cover, clothe, protect. From one of its participle forms, *tectum*, are derived in neo-Latin languages: house, roof, lair. Besides being clearly related to construction and weaving (tecido, tegumento). It also has an extraordinarily rich semantic shade and from it are derived some very interesting groups of words in English as well: tissue, text *et al*.

9. *Walden*, p. 28.

10. *Cf.* Introduction.

11. I will return to that later.

12. *Walden*, pp. 28.

13. *Idem*, p. 81. Elsewhere, in another of Thoreau's poorly read essay, called "*The Landlord*" and devoted to reflecting on some of these problems, he writes: "under one word, house, are included the school house, the jail, the tavern, the dwelling house; and the meanest shed or cave in which men live, contains the elements of all these. But nowhere on the earth stands the entire and perfect house." Thoreau, H. D. *Collected Essays And Poems*. The Library Of America, Vol. 124. New York: The Library Of America, 2001, p. 108.

14. Again, his aristotelianism comes to the fore. As we know, the last and most important of the four causes is the *teleological*, the one which answers the why of something.

15. *Walden*, p. 37.

16. Hesiod and Ovid come immediately to mind and their belief in the ages of gold, silver, bronze and iron.

17. *Walden*, p. 5.

18. *Idem*, p. 45.

19. *Walking*, Thoreau, H. D. *Collected Essays And Poems*. The Library Of America, Vol. 124. New York: The Library Of America, 2001, p. 230.

20. *Walden*, p. 45–46.

21. Aristotle, *Nichomachean Ethics* I, 1, 1094 a, 4–5; VI, 5, 1140 b, 4. *In* Aristotle. *The Basic Works Of Aristotle*. New York: Modern Library, 2001.

22. *Walden*, p. 47.

23. *Idem*, p. 69.

24. *Ibidem*, p. 81.

25. *Ibid.*, p. 46.

26. I will return to that later on in Chapter IV when discussing the more practical aspects of his "Pedagogy of awakening."

27. *Walking, CEP*, p. 231.

28. Thoreau, H. D. *The Journal Of H. D. Thoreau In Fourteen Volumes Bound As Two*. New York: Dover, 1962, vol. XI, p. 386.

29. *Walden*, p. 167 *ff*.

30. *Idem*, p. 166.

31. *Idem*, p. 250.

32. *Ibid.*, p. 64.
33. Thoreau, H. D. *A Week On The Concord And Merrimack Rivers.* Princeton: Princeton University Press, 1980, p. 350.
34. *Walden*, p. 134.
35. *Idem*, p. 115–16.
36. *Ibidem*, p. 116.

Chapter 4

Being Wild

Thoreau's pedagogy of awakening

Nature and awakening. The equation seems certainly odd, considering the efforts of mainstream Western sapiential traditions to extricate us from Nature and transform us into supernatural and special beings. Judeo-Christian, Greek and Modern thinkers, overwhelmingly, have posited a cosmic centrality and finality in our existence that today, when looked at without our deeply ingrained narcissism, can only seem risible and, when believed, ludicrous. There were, however, dissonant voices, since the beginnings, about our true nature and constitution. Voices that could and would not perceive us apart from an elemental constitution, always in deep interdependence with our ultimate dwelling, our habitat, our common house, the cosmos. Unsurprisingly, such a material, elemental and immanent perspective was combined with the utmost awe and fascination that translated into a deeply reverent attitude towards Nature, a sacred outlook that, unfortunately, lies buried beneath the progressive distancing, objectifying and quantitative logocentric approach towards Nature that obnubilates our radicular belonging to Her, resulting in a problematic oblivion of our most archaic dwelling. The question concerning Nature, and our nature, therefore, demands, first and foremost, a genealogical effort in unearthing the many layers of ideological debris that have helped to falsify and distort our perception of both ourselves and Nature. This effort is, I am afraid, fraught with danger and perils, and seems, from the start, considering the many problems involved, one of those unanswerable questions. When one considers the forces that operate against an attempt at addressing that issue: "What is Nature?," one is bound to dejection for, since time immemorial, Nature's ideological twin, Culture, interferes and seems to determine our answers. As we all seem to agree, "Nature" is, after all, a cultural construction. Yet, albeit this knot seems impossible to untie—and I must certainly right now admit to my inability to unravel it—, there still appears to be a relative latitude to considering the possibility that, even dressed up and in the guise in cultural costumes, there remains, in our relationship to Her, something that escapes and transcends our cultural perspectives: our irreplaceable belonging to Her. Outside of words, beyond concepts and beliefs, our physicality, our materiality, our irruption in Her bosom attest to our most embryonic experience, our most archaic dwelling, an incommunicable certainty and truth: we exist, we blossom, we flourish, together with infinite beings and processes, in Nature. Thus, leaving aside, for the time being, any attempt at defining Nature, let us try, here, another approach, an aesthetical and phenomenological one that unfolds in the materialization of some questions: is it possible to retrieve that most archaic experience of belonging? Is it possible to construe a pedagogy towards the realization of that belonging? What might be the possible results of such a path? Unfortunately, this path has its own problems and dangers and, like every ethical demand—for it certainly is an ethical or ethological one, as we shall soon see—seems to lead to other aporias.

Are we free? I'm sorry. I did not want to startle the benevolent but slightly distracted reader and play the Sphinx. Let me rephrase it. Are we capable of submitting our passions, curbing desires and improving on our shortcomings in a deliberate, rational way? Or are we necessarily determined to act as we do because of our innate psycho-physical structures and an overwhelmingly powerful reality? Let's try the middle of the road, then: is it possible to change some things about ourselves, at least? Unfortunately, these questions are far from being rhetorical only; they lie at the very heart of the human ethical and moral endeavor. Humankind has been pondering over those very questions for thousands of years and yet, it looks very far from getting a solution to those answers. The advent of sophisticated technologies and our problematic relationship to Nature seem to multiply infinitely the difficulties of the issue. Free will advocates, determinists, compatibilists—those who go somewhere in the middle of that very large road—all of them are adamant about their respective positions and show a panoply of well-crafted arguments to sustain their viewpoint. Fortunately, we do not need to answer that first, terrible question here. What we do know is that most ethical systems presuppose the very problematic notion of free-will. Fortunately, again, we do not want to go into that maze right now. Maybe we shall have to go further on. What we do want to do now is to investigate how Thoreau dealt with the issue, and typically, true to his perspectivism, there's something in it for every taste. Consider what he writes in the interval of one hundred plus pages in his *Journal*: "who knows how incessant a surveillance a strong man may maintain over himself, how far subject passion and appetite to reason, and lead the life his imagination paints? . . . By a strong effort may he not command even his brute body in unconscious moments?"[1] And this: "What first suggested that necessity was grim, and made fate so fatal? . . . Leave me to my fate . . . I greet thee, my elder brother, who with thy touch ennobles all things. Must it be so, then is it good."[2] Finally: "A great man accepts the occasion the fates offer him. Let us not be disappointed . . . Greatness is in the ascent. But there is no accounting for the little men."[3] Free-will, determinism and compatibilism. The examples could be multiplied throughout his writings.[4] This raises some very interesting questions for us. The first and foremost that comes to my mind is "how can Thoreau say what he says about and to other people's wrong choices and painful states and stations in life if one cannot change one's behavior or ideas/values?" For, if one is simply what one is, how can anyone pretend to be able to teach and change someone else's life? Unless Thoreau is saying that some people are predestined to be free and some aren't in an intriguing, quasi-Calvinist way, we cannot solve this puzzle; and I believe that is exactly what he does. He does not say the "we" are "all" free. He says that "some," "very few" are free. Fated are all: most to be slaves, very few to be free. Why bother to teach, then? Because the ones that are free may ignore they are so and confuse themselves with the slaves. Some, very few, have to be shown that they are free. Most are slaves, to be sure. For them it won't matter anyway, but for those few who are not, it makes the whole difference: "Men talk of freedom! How many are free to think? Free from fear, from perturbation, from prejudice? Nine hundred ninety nine in a thousand are perfect slaves . . . you conquer fate by thought."[5] It is to those very few that Thoreau wants to talk. It is only for the one-in-a-thousand that he is willing to play Chanticleer and give his most precious advice. Yes, I know that the astute reader is thinking: "if all are predestined to be either slaves or free, why bother to teach at all?" Because Thoreau, himself free, was also predestined to teach. Again: "truth is paradoxical."[6] Therefore, it is only for those very, very few that there is a hope and a promise: awakening. It is for those that somehow have the potential, the seed for freedom that Thoreau is going to write what he writes, so that they can find the path, and the pathway for this awakening is the theme of this chapter: Thoreau, the surveyor whose precision was celebrated, is the author of this map, and the map, we shall see, is an extravagant one, through rugged country, making a rough ride, because it is a wild pedagogy.

"We are constantly invited to be what we are,"[7] Thoreau says. Nature, we have seen, is the ground upon which we flourish into existence: we are Nature, according to him. Our singularity is created in a dialogical tension and interdependence with the myriad natural beings and phenomena. Alas, most of the times, we have also seen, we get it wrong about our true identity for a number of reasons: we extract ourselves from Her, superimposing a plethora of ideological and technological paraphernalia between us. Such a regrettable phenomenon—understandable as it is—hampers and jeopardizes our potential for enlightened and ecstatic life. Because of our adventitious misconceptions about ourselves, we lead insincere lives, alienated from Nature and disconnected from our innermost sources of authenticity. Thus, it seems to follow that, if we could somehow manage to reconnect with Nature and engage in a deliberate and sustained effort of self-knowledge, our problems would, theoretically, be over. There is, though, only one very small problem here: what sort of Nature are we talking about? What sort of value are we attaching to Her, so that She becomes our bearing and mirror? Nature, we have seen, is a slippery concept, and even if Thoreau is prepared to sing Nature's perfection, some unanswered questions still linger, such as, what aspects of Nature shall one follow: for a plague, a predator or a tsunami, destructive as they are, are "natural" as well. Shall we behave like them too? Most of us do, as a matter of fact, both individually and collectively. Most are fated—by Nature?—to behave how they do, but, as we have already seen, not all of us are destined to. The problem, thus, seems to be what is natural, innate in us and what is not, *i.e.*, what is cultural, ideological, artificial. And that—I guess on this one everyone agrees—is another typical Sphinx-like question; answer or be devoured. Alas, doubt devours us when we are unable to solve important questions and, to be quite candid, I will be devoured by this one, I guess, since I am acutely aware of being unable to answer that question and solve the problem, unlike the unfortunate Oedipus who, answering correctly the Sphinx's challenge notwithstanding, even so got into terrible troubles.[8] Probably the only sad, pathetic and egotistical consolation is that I am not to be devoured alone. For a number of reasons, that question is a tough one: how could one be capable of disentangling oneself from oneself and observe what oneself truly is? Again, the double challenge "Know thyself and study Nature" seems to point to the need to be conscious of the limits of our knowledge; again, the search, the quest is far more important than a final answer.

Thoreau, however, as we all know, was not the first to say that we should reconnect to or live according to Nature. A sizeable portion of Greek philosophical schools had precisely that as their main tenet: Epicureans[9] and Stoics[10] principally. For both, the main thesis is very similar. We, human beings, are Nature, but a very specific piece of work, or Nature. Her main characteristic, as far as that moral desideratum "to follow Her" is concerned, is that She is, supposedly like us, rational.[11] Although there are major differences between Epicureanism and Stoicism, and minor ones inside Stoicism's several strands, regarding Nature's nature that is a very uncontroversial statement. Nature is rational and so should we also be. We can and should detect how she operates ("Natural laws") and follow, rationally, accordingly. Thus, if we want to be free, wise and happy, we have to follow Her. The problem for us starts exactly here: I cannot recall Thoreau saying that Nature is rational; on the contrary, Nature is free because She is wild. Therefore, our problem remains; how can one follow Nature if one does not understand Her or, worse, in case one understands, is one willing to indulge in an *imitatio naturae* and be prepared to imitate or follow, for instance, a predator or a prey? Again, one has to have a very clear—and positive—conception about what Nature is to be willing to follow Her. So, it appears to be the case that, according to Thoreau, if we want to be happy and free, we are invited to be wild: to "take a walk on the wild side." Hence, it seems that our best course of action is to try to figure out "what is wild"—and that, as we will soon discover, is a synonym of the good.

"How near to good is what is wild! Life consists with wildness. The most alive is the wildest. Not yet subdued to man, its presence refreshes him."[12] Wild is good, tame is bad: that is a fundamental equation for Thoreau. The more domesticated, the more civilized, the worst; the wilder, the best. We lead artificial, corrupted lives because we have distanced ourselves from the source, from the living dynamics of the web of life. The many layers of cultural varnish that both society and we apply all over ourselves cripple our true vitality and veil the most profound, radical, subterranean fountains of our existential vigor. It dries the sap, congealing the marrow of life. That distancing spells a misunderstanding about the nature of some of us and our original belonging to the wilderness as well. And here we face a double challenge from which there is no avoiding. The first one has to do with the necessary domestication of humans. There is no civilization without domestication, Thoreau knows that; so how can he propose a "return to wildness," to a more intimate relationship with Nature, when he knows that most of us have a tendency towards tameness?

> "I rejoice that horses and steers have to be broken before they can be made slaves of men, and that men themselves have some wild oats still left to sow before they become submissive members of society. Undoubtedly all men are not equally fit subjects for civilization, and because the majority, like dogs and sheep, are tame by inherited disposition, is no reason the others should have their natures broken."[13]

To be broken, as Thoreau emphasizes, is the decisive civilizational baptism that integrates one into society. It is the rite of passage that degrades one from one's natural state into a civilized stage. The "breaking," that domesticating process, though, is not for everyone. Some are fitted to it because of their innate nature, their inherited disposition. Most are born to be civilized slaves, and here Thoreau's fatalistic quasi-Calvinist determinism appears again. Most will never hear nor heed "the call of the wild," as Jack London beautifully puts it. Most of us are destined to live our small lives of "quiet desperation," but for the few, for those who might be only misguided about their real nature, the call is very important because it awakens what was deeply asleep inside ourselves. It reawakens us from the oblivion towards the quest, the search for us "to become who we really and already are," to use Pindar's felicitous phrase adopted by Thoreau. Thus, the map to awakening, the pedagogy of the wilderness I am about to articulate should be seen necessarily as a roadmap to only a few of us. It is irrelevant here to wonder about "why" most are born to be slaves and some aren't: we would have to pretend to have a privileged access to the very heart of cosmic organization to know that which, obviously, is not the case, at least in my case. We have just seen how architecture and agriculture are instantiations of the civilizing process that domesticates all and sundry. However, it seems that, according to Thoreau, some beings, humans included, are more domesticated than others. Some are heavy sleepers, others, not that much. Some might awaken, most are beyond the pale. Therefore, the path we are on the verge of treading must be a priori considered to be only for very few, undemocratic as it may sound. That is a very important premise.

The second point to bear in mind is that when I use the term wild, I really mean it. Wild means savage, untamed, and unpalatable to those more domestic creatures: rough, rugged, hard. We shall later see that "the wild" is not only natural wilderness, but it is also present in literature, politics, the social and individual dimensions as well. There is no middle of the road here because, as we have seen before, the mean is for the mediocre. It is a radical path, an earth-rooted spring of life. A natural way of being and acting, and here there seems to sprout an apparent contradiction: we are also cultural creatures, Thoreau's opinion notwithstanding. This seems to be our particularly human predicament: a hybrid being of culture and Nature. What is Nature? What is Culture? Those questions, as I have been trying to underline, seem to me to be unsolvable puzzles; for me, not for Thoreau, mind you: "Nature and man: some prefer the one, others the other; but that is all *de gustibus.* It makes no odds at what well you drink, provided it is a well-head."[14] One can find Nature inside the human and the human within Nature, provided one drinks at the right fountain, self-knowledge: individual human self-knowledge is one of Nature's shortcuts towards awareness of Her own Self. However, most are fated to be slaves in society and few are to be free in Nature, but right now we are only concerned with the very, very few. And then, pops the question up: aren't they—those very, very few—cultural beings as well? If not, how can one find out that one is alienated from Nature? Certainly not within Nature Herself, otherwise one would not be distant and alienated from Her. Thus, it becomes clear that it is only from within the realm of Culture that our peculiar alienated position can be discerned. It takes immersion in society to discover we are Nature! It takes distance from Nature to perceive we are Nature, as Thoreau probably realized amidst his fellow Concordians. Cultural, societal existence is the unique absolute condition of possibility towards realizing our original natural condition. It is only from the perspective of distance that a rapport with the collective of Nature is possible. That is why Thoreau is capable of detecting the problem, because he lives at the border between Nature and culture: "For my part, I feel that with regard to Nature I live a sort of border life, on the confines of a world into which I make occasional and transient forays only, and my patriotism and allegiances to the State into whose territories I seem to retreat are those of the moss-trooper."[15] The venturesome nature of Thoreau's forays into Nature allows him to question his allegiances in terms of the dichotomy Nature versus Culture. His border life is a frontier life, with one foot solidly planted in Concord/Culture, whilst the other foot saunters through the woods. One might even call it contradictory if one is not able to appreciate both his perspectivism and his capacity to appreciate civilization's best fruits: however, he leaves no doubt whatsoever as to his true calling: "I feel that I draw nearest to understanding the great secret of my life in my closest intercourse with nature. There is a reality and health in (present) nature; which is not to be found in any religion—and cannot be contemplated in antiquity—I suppose that what in other men is religion is in me love of nature."[16] The ideological cornerstone of the way is passionately laid out: self/Nature-understanding comes with intimacy with Nature and that, for him, is sacredness itself. Religion, the *re-ligare* ("reconnect") here is naturalized. The naturalization of the supernatural is a stupendous shift from a tradition that overvalues the beyond and relegates the natural and material world to a subaltern position. That naturalization subverts the old dualistic approach and reveals one of the most important features of an immanent, non-dual perspective on existence. The longing look that alights on the landscapes of Nature becomes a look on the body of the Divine: theology becomes physics and botany and chemistry, theodicy. Intimacy with the natural world upends our cultural inherited values inasmuch as it dissolves the ingrained duality of "us and the Other" reconfiguring our glance to be able to witness the fluid and interdependent ballet of the Whole, blurring the dichotomies between "self and non-self." Our domesticated views become wild vistas, enlarged and suffused with the shining component of the *theion*, the divine, vivifying what once was natural—whether subaltern, dead or dangerous and strange—into a vibrant and pulsating totality, a cosmic dance in which our psycho-physical frame is engulfed by an undulating high tide of Nature's sentience. Not even the arcane proximity of ancient societies to the pristine human condition can surpass the immediacy of the lace of conscious light that one may experience in the embrace of Nature: the embrace of the Maiden, as he calls Her. That love of Nature—*physiophilia*—is both philosophy and physiology: it is Natural Philosophy potentiated by aesthetical and ecstatic radicalism, the integrative experience with the single root of Being and its infinite branches. The ideal look becomes a necessarily inter- and trans-disciplinary holistic approach that galvanizes mythopoetic diction, qualified and quantified data in an alternative epistemological tress that nomadically shifts its perspective to capture a richer and more diversified palette of hues that can better delineate the contours of phenomena, so that "truths" become "perspectives" and "grace," "breathing," a healthy breathing, since it marks the confluence of the rhythm of the individual breathing with the systole and diastole of the All, whose auscultation can be carried on with the Emersonian stethoscope of "Know thyself and study Nature." That ideal look is transformed into method, an extra-vagant sauntering, a going beyond the accepted and safe perimeter that refuses complicity with the sclerotic and domesticated biases that fence the wilderness of truth and beauty off from tamed civilization.

But religion, according to some ancients and Cicero in particular,[17] is not only *re-ligare*, ("reconnect") but can also be a *re-legere* ("reread," that is, "to read with attention, care and intensively"): in Thoreau's case a rereading of the book of Nature, a sustained, careful and caring look that judges not, but tries to accept, for only acceptance entails understanding and only understanding unveils the patterns which allow us to harmonize with Her, creating that healthy and serene wellness that percolates through the porous membranes separating the interconnected bodies within Her embracing totality. It is also a reading of the presence of wilderness in literature and mythology:

> "In literature it is only the wild that attracts us. Dullness is only another name for tameness. It is the untamed, uncivilized, free and wild thinking in Hamlet, in the Iliad, and in all scriptures and mythologies that delight us, not learned in the schools, not refined and polished by art. A truly good book is something as wildly natural and primitive, mysterious and marvelous, ambrosial and fertile, as a fungus or lichen."[18]

The "wild," as we can see, is not only natural wilderness. It is also the recondite fountain, the source from where the new emerges. Civilization is tame. Tame is dull because it engages in the never-ending vicious circle of reasserting its domesticated and domesticating impoverishing values. Such tautological axiology is boring in its self-assertiveness and self-righteous ruminating virtues. The unhewn word, the savage thought injects vitality in art and morphs a cultural product into a wildness manifesto. This "wild" reading is a sort of magical wand that can transport us to those regions still virgin to the reins of social mores and thence it is still possible to expect the ever-renewing surge of creativity that opposes the spontaneity of the creators to the restraint of society's creatures. That is why Homer, Virgil and Shakespeare smell of wilderness. Beauty, vigor—the Good—is wild. On the other hand, that autistic social morality not only jeopardizes creativity but goes out of its way to literally punish those it considers deviants. Moreover, it is the influx of the wild that founds social dissent, an axiomatic principle of plural societies that see difference as intrinsic richness. Conventional art is tame and boring because it does not challenge us anymore and assuages our doubts and fears. The choice of fungus and lichen to figuratively compare with a good work of art is fascinating: both live on a limbo between the mineral and the vegetable world: so is good, wild art, a unique mix of Culture, the form, and Nature, the wild. Good literature/art is not contrived, it does not instrumentalize art towards a moralistic end; it prods and makes us uncomfortable, it excites and challenges us. It is alive. It is wild. Most literature, alas, like humankind, is tame:

> "Where is the literature which gives expression to Nature? He would be a poet who could impress the winds and streams into his service, to speak for him; ... transplanted them to his page with earth adhering to their roots; whose words were so true and fresh and natural that they would appear to expand like buds at the approach of Spring ... in sympathy with surrounding Nature ... I do not know of any poetry to quote which adequately expresses this yearning for the Wild. Approached from this side, the best poetry is tame ... I demand something that something which no culture, in short, can give ... Mythology comes nearer to it than anything. How much more fertile a Nature, at least, has Grecian mythology its roots in."[19]

This excerpt unearths multiple roots of Thoreau's wildest philosophical and aesthetical ideals and, once again, it is mythology, specifically the Greek one that better translates his taste. Archaic Greece is a special time and place for Thoreau. It is redolent of the freshness of the youth of humankind's still-vigorous thought and poetry. We can almost see him with the Iliad—by far his favorite book[20]—on his lap by Walden dreaming of his Arcadian Greece. His devotion to Greek archaic thinkers and poets is perfectly comprehensible. Their holistic Natural Philosophy entitles them to be named archaic: they are near the *arche*, the original source and fountain of Western wisdom, science, poetry and mythology, some of the same springs to which Thoreau will dedicate most of his efforts and abilities. His love for that select group of poets and thinkers is amply justified. They have laid profoundly and solidly the piles of Western thought. Experience-wise, they are still in sympathy, in communion with the wilderness, with the still undomesticated and radical demand of intelligibility of an unknown Physis, the still untamed vigor of knowledge. Their eyes were still blank with innocence, unlike ours, opaque by the films of tradition. They were thinkers who wrote mythopoetically, the sacred language itself, and could decipher Nature's hyerogliphs. They were still virgins to the domestication of knowledge that splits in different registers their total view of reality: one foot in science, the other one in mythology and celebrated as divine poets/writers like Homer, Hesiod, Orpheus, Pythagoras, Empedocles, Aeschylus, Euripides, Plato and so many others—all of them companions of Thoreau and subjects of his reflection. They are foundational thinkers, mythographers and poets who could see the *holos,* the Whole, still wild, still agrestic, still vigorous. Their eyes could still capture all the freshness of the luminous diaphanous lace of Nature thinking Herself, their views flourishing like those elegant pines on the copper cliffs sculpted by Boreas and licked by the turquoise of the Egean Sea. Their views, today buried deeper than the fragmented elegant Doric columns of the ancient temples that floated in marble over the sacred woods of the Gods, remain a perpetual challenge to our reductionist and wretched way of segmenting the All, the totality of what is, into bits and pieces of disjointed and disconnected splinters by some antiquarian's verbose ineptudes: to sing Nature, the Whole, in poetry, science, myth and philosophy, that is the pedagogy of the Wilderness:

> "No one sees nature, who sees her not as young and fresh, without history. We may have such intercourse today as we imagine to constitute the employment of gods. We live here to have intercourse with rivers, forests, mountains—beasts and men. How few do we see conversing with these things. We think the ancients were foolish who worshipped the sun. I would worship it forever if I had grace to do so":[21]

To worship the wild and make it explicit in as many ways possible, since it lies veiled and implicit in our techno and idiocratic brave new world. To unveil the infinite faces of Nature:

> "Here is this vast, savage, howling mother of ours, Nature, lying all around, with such beauty, and such affection for her children . . . and yet we are so early weaned from her breast to society, to that culture which is exclusively an interaction of man and man—a sort of breeding in and in . . . give me a culture which imports much muck from the meadows, and deepens the soil."[22]

Our savage mother is the only one capable of still fertilizing the best possible culture; only a wild culture, a wild cultivation, a wild pedagogy can still redeem us from the narcoleptic state of a technocratic civilization that not only does not care for the wild but diligently deforms it through unrelenting hatred for the other that refuses to yield; where only utter and complete destruction will do. Domestication, tameness, submission or destruction: hasn't this been the most amply adopted political mantra that has historically founded human political action towards the many others: humans or Nature? For those who want to build a narcissistic mirror for culture based on Nature, Thoreau has some very strong words:

"While almost all men feel an attraction drawing them to society, few are attracted enough to Nature. In their relation to Nature men appear to me for the most part, notwithstanding their art, lower than the animals. It is not often a beautiful relation, as in the case of the animals. How little appreciation of the beauty of the landscape there is among us! We have to be told that the Greeks called the world κόσμος (cosmos), Beauty, or Order, but we do not see clearly why they did so."[23]

Notwithstanding their arts, their techniques, they are degraded to a lower-than-animal existence. Their alienation not only corrupts Nature, it degrades them to a bestial life. The unexpected inversion is fascinating: technology bestializes humans into sub-animalistic dimensions! That double deformation of Nature and themselves entails the peculiar narcissistic blunder that it is only technology that can heal our most profound wounds. That is patently absurd, for how can an instrument heal alienated Nature of Herself? How can technique introduce us to that anamnetic process of self-knowledge? It cannot. Only philosophy, poetry and intimacy with Nature can. Unless, of course, one develops a very peculiarly tame and domesticated view of Nature, that is, a completely artificial and false simulacrum out of it, so that we can pretend to fill out a hole by digging another one. In his own prescient, unique prophetic way, Thoreau shows how technique itself becomes the instrument of their debasement, since it is technique that allows them to distance themselves from Nature and deform the landscape, domesticating it to nefarious ends. Such a perversion blinds us to the most sublime aspects of reality. Once again, the Greeks come to the fore, because of their still wild innocence. We, ourselves, cannot see how they could see such a beauty. Nature was there and She is still here; what we have lost was the innocent, the wild look, that wonder towards the unsurpassed perfection and beauty of reality. That is why a "wild pedagogy" is also, necessarily, a "pedagogy of the look": a cultivation of the way one looks at the Other. It is the eye, the uncultivated eye that deforms and kills before the technique or the weapon; to be capable of dismantling the ideological constructs that have domesticated our vision until the point of inanity; an eye-care, literally: the possibility of retrieving that almost lost Greek, infantile awe-filled glance onto the landscape. The very idea of "landscape" is, in itself, instructive: the result of the encounter of the eye with the Other, the digestion of the dynamics of the time-space fluid frame; in our case, the deformed landscapes of deforming imaginations. To accept and respect the "Other-Nature" as an axiomatic presupposition to a new—which is in fact archaic—wild look, one has to shift one's perspective: "men nowhere, east or west, live yet a natural life, round which the vine clings, and which the elm willingly shadows. Man would desecrate it by his touch, and so the beauty of the world remains veiled to him.

He needs not only to be spiritualized, but naturalized on the soil of earth."[24] Thoreau stresses the urgency to change the parameters: we do not need spirit, we need Nature! Western's religious tradition is overly emphatic as to the supposed causes of our woes: lack of "spiritualization" and "philanthropy," among others. Nothing could be more distant from Henry's perspective; love of "spirit" in inversely proportional to distancing from "earth." We need a new spirituality, one that does not divide and amputate beings from Nature. More than a "Heaven," he seems to be pointing to the need of a sacralization of Earth, of Nature. The long history of the divide between us and Nature replicates our distancing from our fellow humans. According to that new belief, which abandons the protocols of inertial weight, there is no need for churches; the wild will do if we are able to transform our look. This shift, though, is extraordinarily difficult to achieve because of the immemorial deformation and defamation of Nature: "he's an animal," "she's wild," "x is a stone," "a viper" etc. The list of negative figurative comparisons would be endless. That is why Thoreau will underline the imperative need to a radical change of perspective, what I have called his perspectivism: "there are innumerable avenues to a perception of the truth . . . probe the universe in a myriad points . . . he is a wise man and experienced who has taken many views; to whom stones and plants and animals and a myriad objects have each suggested something, contributed something."[25] Instead of the quintessential Christian "brotherly and neighborly love," a new catechism: "I wish my neighbors were wilder. A wilderness no civilization could endure . . . Live free, child of the mist . . . for man is superior to all laws, both of heaven and earth . . . wild as if we lived on the marrow of antelopes devoured raw."[26] Now, that is amazing, *extravagant*, really. The invitation to assume a new view, a new gospel, brings with it the need to eschew the old ones. To create new idols one has to smash the old ones, as Nietzsche was to say some decades after Thoreau. Instead of pleading for peace, love and harmony, a paean to wilderness! Instead of a holy waffle, to devour raw antelope marrow! How wilder can it get? But one might say, and say well: "but if we all lived like Nature, would it not be chaos?" Hobbes' classical formulation of the State of Nature as the general war of all against all immediately comes to mind with its supposed horrific consequences: we have been told so. And here Thoreau most definitely parts company from Aristotle, Hobbes, Locke, Montesquieu and most classical political writers who have written on the "social compact" that supposedly would have transferred us from the "state of nature" to the "political state"; from Rousseau, the differences are fewer but even so enormous. Rousseau never advocated a "return to Nature" as explicitly as Thoreau does. Besides, and maybe most importantly, I don't think Thoreau is interested in solving any problems: religious, political or otherwise; I guess he is basically concerned with raising awareness by presenting us a really new, fresh perspective on things that is, also, therapeutic; that is why his alternative is a much more radical one: "in short, all good things are wild and free . . . give me for friends and neighbors wild men, not tame ones. The wildness of the savage is but a faint symbol of the awful ferity with which good men and lovers meet."[27] It is fascinating to note how Thoreau juxtaposes "the Good" with "the Wild" escaping from millennia of indoctrination that approximates "Good" with either "God," "Reason" or "Virtue" and, more interesting still, how he notes that "savagery"—in the best possible sense—is still among and inside us in our most decisively human moments, after all: "you have a wild savage in you";[28] this savage that lies dormant inside us is the fountain whence creativity may surge, where regeneration and renewal is to be found. It is that savage inside us that he is trying to awaken; but how could we possibly do that? It is time to turn to specifics.

"Walden—Yesterday I came here to live. My house makes me think of some mountain houses I have seen, which seemed to have a fresh auroreal atmosphere about them, as I fancy of the halls of Olympus."[29] Those are the very first words written by Thoreau at Walden Pond on July, 5th 1845, after spending his first night at his cabin. Interestingly, "wildness" (= Walden), "auroreal"="dawn" and Olympus, the home of the Greek Divines, are related. The freshness of the wild, of the awakening hour of the day and the home of the divines of his beloved Greece get entwined and are seen from a culturally constructed viewpoint, a house, his dwelling. His hut, his social minimum, his burrow, was to become his outermost clothing, a thin and malleable fluid membrane that marginally deformed the landscape and did not separated him from Nature, rather, as he would say later on, encaged him inside Her. Apart from everything else that might be said about his going to Walden, there is no denying that his "experiment" is, first and foremost, a getting closer to Nature, an approximation and more: a returning. Walden Pond and its woods are among his first memories, Thoreau having been previously there when he was still a child. Therefore, he is not only returning to Walden. He is returning to an apparently lost world of innocent wonder and wilderness, exactly the two pivots around which his life—and his wild pedagogy—would thenceforth gravitate. He is embarking, thus, on an anamnetic journey not only towards his past; far more important, he is embarking on an adventure towards *arche*, the origin, the genesis, the wilderness within, an interior dawn, a golden Greek beginning. Somewhere down on the woods' paths of his memories lies the savage he was trying to connect not only genealogically but, principally, ontologically; that lost Greek look, that lost kid's awe—the savage was there, he felt, lurking somewhere inside him. Outside, down on the woods' paths lies Nature. By the end of his sojourn at Walden, he was to discover that there was no inside and no outside within Her, but that would come later on: first things first. The goal he was aiming at through that intimacy with Nature is explicit in the immediately next entry of his journal, July 6th:

> "I wish to meet the facts of life—the vital facts, which are the phenomena or actuality the Gods meant to show us—face to face, and so I came down here . . . in all studies we go not forward but rather backward with redoubled pauses. We always study antiques with pause and reflection. Even time has a depth, and below its surface the waves do not lapse and roar . . . —one emancipated heart and intellect! It would knock off the fetters from a million slaves."[30]

The most important facts of life, those divine ones which the Gods—not God, mind you—want to show us: wisdom, serenity, fruits of that genealogical anamnetic itinerary, lie beneath and beyond temporality in a realm of awakened freedom. An awakening that might multiply exponentially, shattering social, political, economical and spiritual bonds that bounded all sorts of slaves, and many a type they were. Suspended above Time but deeply rooted in Nature, Thoreau will slowly and dexterously weave his soteriological agenda; the first point, immersion in wilderness.

> "To insure health, a man's relation to Nature must come very near to a personal one; he must be conscious of a friendliness in her . . . I cannot conceive of any life which deserves the name, unless there is a certain tender relation to Nature . . . unless Nature sympathizes with and speaks to us, as it were, the most fertile and blooming regions are barren and dreary."[31]

Love of Nature and friendship with Her—*physiophilia*—is the condition *sine qua non* for starting the adventure of self and Nature knowledge. Intimacy manifests itself in mute accordance, the silent harmony that does not need to be explained or articulated. However, it must be a two-way road: our friendship with Her and Her sympathy with us. Her sympathy with us is given, but our proximity to Her exacts an effort from us, since our long-gone nearness to Her is just an exiled longing. The effort is also necessary to overcome Her defamation and our misunderstandings about ourselves. Maybe forced in the beginning, nearness engenders familiarity, then intimacy; but if intimacy is not mutual, it is not intimacy but accompanied solitude. The demanded tenderness is the human counterpart of the radicle's soft vigor and connection to earth. We may imagine that in the beginning, the contact of a budding root with earth may not be comfortable: earth probably resists, but as contact and co-terminality grow, borders and limits melt. We are not plants, though, albeit also being related to them: cousins, no less; in that familiar intimacy not everything is said, the unsaid being perfectly felt. Tenderness, friendship, sympathy and love engender life, and life far from Nature is not life properly, but a slow death. The death of fertility: sclerotic culture. Healthiness, wellness can only be found at the source, where life blooms. Intimacy with Nature teaches one how to accord with Her. They way to fertility and bloom lies in connecting to Nature, both inside and outside us.

"Next to Nature, it seems as if man's actions were the most natural, they so gently accord with her."[32] We are Nature, but of a very special type. A type of Nature who forgets it is Nature, thus, as a starter, the first demand is necessarily a step back, and not one forward; in that therapeutic anamnesis, in order to advance, we must be prepared, first, to return: a return to Her bosom. There, in sympathy, in communion, one may start to discern Her moods and traits, cycles and ruptures, creation and destruction, incorporating this fierce wisdom to our praxis. More important, studying Her, we can discover who we really are:

"how important is a constant intercourse with nature and the contemplation of natural phenomena to the preservation of moral and intellectual health . . . The philosopher contemplates human affairs as calmly and from as great a remoteness as he does natural phenomena. The ethical philosopher needs the discipline of the natural philosopher. He approaches the study of mankind with great advantages who is accustomed to the study of nature."[33]

Packed here lie some remarkable orientations about his methodology, contents and ends. In fact, the whole project of Natural Philosophy is laid bare in those few lines. Thoreau's synthesis delimits the radium and reach of his method: intercourse with Nature, Her contemplation and self-contemplation, repeating myself—"Gnothi sauton and study Nature." The two goals are not different, they are simply different stages of the same "therapeia," in Greek: care, attention, healing; three fundamental words of Henry's vocabulary. "Intimacy with Nature" means care, attention and healing: method, goal and result in a nutshell. To study humans as integrally "Nature," ethologically, is not only tremendously sophisticated methodology, it is downright revolutionary today. His sensibility in terms of transferring to everything human the then unheard-of ethological model demonstrates Thoreau's extraordinary ecological perception and, Wallace and Darwin's revolutionary Biology notwithstanding, Thoreau's combination of Natural Philosophy, self-knowledge, politics, poetry, myth, history *et al*, amplifies significantly the scope of a purely biological approach to the human phenomenon, embracing art, wisdom and science in an natural, anthropocosmic, holistic philosophy that, idiosyncratic as it may seem, presents us with the double challenge of therapeutic self-knowledge and caring intimacy with Nature, whose method, contents, scope and result could certainly be regarded as revolutionary as well: the scenery, when it is truly seen, reacts on the life of the seer. "How to live. How to get the most of life. As you were to teach the younger hunter how to entrap his game. How to extract its honey from the flower of the world. That is my everyday business."[34] And an amazing business it is. The interdependent complementariness of landscape and eye, of both subject and object, when correctly observed, both as non-dual modes of Nature, opens a magnificent window of opportunity towards natural, wild pedagogies. Nature teaches one how to live. As a hunter learns to entrap, Thoreau learns to extract honey from the very same Teacher. An intimate, caring and attentive look is also openness to the Other, an openness that must attend in vigil to learn to transform the simple acts of life into theurgic empowerment, when the prosaic turns epiphanic. The distance from both extremes of the band of potential human experience is bridged and overcome by that aware openness that does not relegate the Other—whomever or whatever the Other happens to be—to a subaltern position: the Other can teach us if, and only if, we are willing to engage intimately Her or him or it, with care and attention: "No method or discipline can supersede the necessity of being forever on the alert. What is a course of history, philosophy, or poetry, no matter how well selected, or the best society, or the most admirable routine of life, compared with the discipline of looking always at what is to be seen."[35] A wild pedagogy, as stated earlier, is perforce a pedagogy of the look. However, in this case, it is also at the first stages necessarily negative: one has to unlearn how one looks at things so that the obsidian of our pupils becomes once again transparent: a transparent crystal globe, as Thoreau's guru, Emerson, might have said. The inevitability of the look, the iron bond that connects subject and object, ought to be tended with a special collyrium, though: attention. Our unfocused, impatient glance does not have the discipline to really look and see. Neither the arts and humanities nor society or routine can replace the sympathetic openness and patience that the empty look demands. Empty, not vacuous, since vacuous is the look that cannot see through the many ideological layers that have, hitherto, deformed the viewer, the viewing and the view: "How much virtue there is in simply seeing! . . . [We] are as much as we see. Faith is sight and knowledge. The hands only serve the eyes . . . ; what I saw alters not."[36] Our identity is construed by what we have seen, for to be able to *see* means to be already sympathetically connected and open to the Other: it is this dialogical tension of the landscape and the eye that shapes us and feeds us:

> "All this you will see, and much more, if you are prepared to see it,—if you look it . . . objects are concealed from our view not so much because they are out of the course of our visual ray as because there is no intention of the mind and eye toward them . . . we do not realize how far and wide, or how near and narrowly, we are to look. The greater part of the phenomena of nature are for this reason concealed from us . . . there is just as much beauty visible to us in the landscape

as we are prepared to appreciate,—not a grain more . . . the scarlet oak must, in a sense, be in your eye when you go forth. We cannot see anything until we are possessed with the idea of it, and then we can hardly see anything else."[37]

This extraordinary claim reminds one of Anaxagoras' (500/428 b.c.e.) most famous theses: that everything contains, in some way, everything else. Aristotle was to call that mutual pollination *homeomeries*, "homogeneous substances." It is fascinating to imagine that Thoreau arrived at the same conclusion without coming into contact with his thought, although he might have had the chance of getting somehow acquainted with it through the works of Aëtius. The correlation between the eye and the landscape seems to be prearranged by the presence of an image somehow inside the looker's vision or consciousness. In some way it seems to point to an anamnetic preview of the object in a quasi-Platonic theory of the ideas, where we somehow get in touch with the eternal ideal correlates of things before we incarnate. Though far-fetched in this sense, Thoreau's relationship with metempsychosis (*grosso modo* "reincarnation") is intriguing and begs for a closer inspection. Be that as it may, that radical intentionality advocated by Thoreau is explicit enough. We do not see things because we do not recognize them. This is also ancient Philosophy and the Stoics were known to say that without a previous "preconception, prolepse" (*prolepsis*) we would not be able to get in touch with things in general, since we would not be able to recognize had we not had previously been somehow unconsciously and innately acquainted with them. Here, Thoreau's perspective seems to allude to a pre-arrangement or necessitating previous accordance between the subject and the object. It is mesmerizing to try to imagine how Thoreau might have articulated that infinite hall of mirrors, where images were to be previously found in the eye, bending time-space orthodox relationships. This recognition, incidentally, might throw some light on his notion of "sympathy," literally, a "conjoint affection," this sui generis relationship between subjects and objects.

That eye-object "ocular sympathy" is also the optimum result of a previous topical rearrangement of our look: from within, from introspective self-knowledge, the key to a propedeutic inherited and deforming ideological disassemble, to the outside, to Nature. It is necessary to look hard and deep into the abyss of oneself to be able to detect and clarify the falsifying and deforming films of tradition; the shift from that inward look to the outward marks the ideal cleansing of the retina from the patina of the sclerotic garbage of tradition. From the internal to the external, the way to wisdom: "The art of life! Was there anything memorable written upon it? By what discipline to secure the most life, with what care to watch our thoughts. To observe what transpires, not in the street, but in the mind and heart of me!"[38] Thoreau's continuous exercise of self-search demands a sustained tension between interior awareness and external observation, both, ultimately, translating into care. That discipline is an everlasting one, the important thing being, as we well remember, the quest itself:

> "Let me forever go in search of myself; never for a moment think that I have found myself; be as a stranger to myself, never a familiar, seeking acquaintance still. May I be to myself as one to me whom I love, a dear and cherished object. What temple, what fane, what sacred place can there be but the innermost part of my own being. The possibility of my own improvement, that is to be cherished."

From Delphi's marbles walls to Freud's divan, "*Gnothi sauton*," "know thyself," has been one of the most important practices of self-care of the Western world. The invitation for us to know ourselves lies at the very basis of Western philosophy and it is celebrated as the best tool to achieve serenity and wisdom. The result of the discipline has been variously interpreted: "know your limits," "know you are not a God," "cultivate yourself." Together with the other Delphic maxim "*meden agan*," "nothing in excess," they form the nucleus of Western classical wisdom; the unanimous convergence of all diverse traditions and schools of thought, that recipe for eudaimonia cannot be seen as an egotistical self-centeredness. On the contrary, as Thoreau himself explains in the sequel of the above quote, self-knowledge is fundamental not only to "know who we really are"; as Thoreau remarked the project is open-ended and inconclusive, but it is also extraordinarily important in terms of self-transformation and intersubjective relationships: "Oh my dear friends, I have not forgotten you. I will know you tomorrow. I associate with you my ideal self."[39] Self-knowledge is a propedeutic, prophylactic measure that helps that cleansing process: first to know ourselves, and then get acquainted with the Other, already transformed, already relatively freed from the burden of tradition. It is decisive to know who we really are first and, in the process, to better and prepare ourselves for a more convivial and fraternal relationship with the Other, whoever or whatever that might be. In this light, self-knowledge is a political instrument as well, in as much as it produces a better neighbor, citizen and fellow human being. Self-knowledge is, therefore, an exploration of the unknown inside of us, an adventure to those interior wildernesses which we most of the times do not dare to face, nor visit. It is a sauntering towards our interior outback and dark woods: self-knowledge is wild pedagogy too, as Thoreau puts it in the concluding pages of Walden, commenting on a stanza by William Habington:[40]

> "What does Africa,—what does the West stand for? Is not our own interior white on the chart? Black though it may prove, like the coast, when discovered

... [If] you would travel farther than all travelers, be naturalized in all climes, and cause the Sphynx to dash her head against a stone, even obey the precept of the old philosopher and Explore thyself. Herein are demanded the eye and the nerve."[41]

This is rich, isn't it? Our uncharted interior white spots, like nineteenth century maps, may even prove to be black when charted, however, according to Thoreau, "the surveyor," to travel really far one has to turn one's gaze within. That is the biggest challenge and the most rewarding discovery of all. The Sphynx appears again, this time ashamed and herself defeated by the introspective adventurer. She will not devour the self-explorer. Only the eye and the nerve are necessary to the Argonaut of the spirit; the courage to really look and see. Eye and nerve are the only two necessary pieces of the anatomy one has to use. Self-knowledge is not easy, it hurts; yes, I know it sounds like more than dubious sugary self-help, but it is plain it pains us to change and grow. It shows oneself what one truly is: the white spot may prove to be black, unknown, uncharted psychic territory. Moreover, there is no return ticket, it is an endless journey—bridges and ships are burned; once one dives into the dark interior waters, there is no going back: "In spaces of thought are the reaches of land and water, where man go and come. The landscape lies far and far within and the deepest thinker is the farthest travelled."[42] We have already heard Heraclitus saying "Nature likes to hide": ours to ourselves probably much more so. But he also said "I searched into myself,"[43] "All men have the capacity of knowing themselves and acting with moderation"[44] and "You could not in your going find the ends of the soul, though you travelled the whole way."[45] From the wise man of Ephesus, who lived in the sacred woods of Artemis playing ball with the kids, to the forest sage of Concord who lived in the sacred woods of Walden running huckleberry parties with the kids: the abyss of the soul is exactly the same, yet completely different. The vertigo of the experience, idem.

However, such nearness to, and investigation of both our own selves and Nature comes with a price-tag: "By my intimacy with Nature I find myself withdrawn from man. My interest in the sun and the moon, in the morning and evening, compels me to solitude."[46] Apparently, a price Thoreau was only too willing to pay, as he wonders:

"Why should I feel lonely? Is not our planet in the Milky-Way? . . . What sort of space is that which separates a man from his fellows and make him solitary? . . . What do we want most to dwell near to? Not to many men surely, the depot, the post-office, the bar-room, the meeting-house, the school-house, the grocery, Beacon Hill . . . where men most congregate, but to the perennial source of our life . . . as the willow stands near the water and sends its roots in that direction."[47]

What seems to separate Thoreau from his fellow human beings is not physical distance itself, but a certain idea of proximity. Proximity is distance when two cannot agree as to the importance of proximity to what is really important. Henry wanted proximity to what he perceived as the perennial source of life: wild Nature; besides, there is no company as good as solitude: "I love to be alone. I never found the companion that was so companionable as solitude."[48] However, as we have just seen, there is wilderness both inside and outside of us. The same fresh source that wild Nature represents outside of us exists within us as well, to be approached by self-knowledge. Moreover, wilderness exists in society too. Micro (individual), meso (society) and macro (Nature) wildernesses: one discovers that the wild is a dimension that cuts through every region of reality. In a tame society, wilderness has another name: dissent.

"All men recognize the right of revolution; that is, the right to refuse allegiance to, and resist, the government, when its tyranny or its inefficiency are great and unendurable."[49] All over the New World, the first political experiences were born in the wilderness, in the meeting of the eyes of the wild natives and the eyes of the savage conquistadores; a fierce encounter by all means, in an impossible wildness, far beyond Europe's maddest and wildest imagination. In due time, many tears were to be shed from both eyes, much more from the wild natives' who refused domestication and preferred death, that ultimate wilderness, the ultimate unchartered unknown. In the northern part of America, a handful of wild dreamers in the wildernesses of New England decided to resist the most powerful Empire the world had ever seen. America was born of a wild dream, not on a fence—or wall. Alas, wildly beautiful and glorious revolutions grow tame in time. By Thoreau's epoch it was not only domesticated, it was domesticating others, landscapes and peoples. "Under a government which imprisons any unjustly, the true place for a just man is also a prison . . . [;] it is here that the fugitive slave, and the Mexican prisoner on parole, and the Indian come to plead the wrongs of his race."[50] Slavery, robbing Mexico and exterminating Indians;[51] violence against Blacks, Latinos and Native Americans: sounds familiar? It does. There and here, Thoreau demonstrates that political action in a sclerotic society must necessarily stem from dissent, from revolt, to question the tame, self-complacent domesticated status quo: a demonstration that Mahatma Gandhi and Martin Luther King, Jr. heeded. To disobey the establishment is to obey Democracy; to disobey dominium, non-cooperation. To confront tameness, wildness, as Captain John Brown and Thoreau were to show in different and complementary ways.[52] There must be Thoreauvian savages to fertilize Democracy opposing corrupt and predatory Capitalism. Every single step towards Democratic fulfillment, towards Economic, Political and Social equality and Humanistic Justice comes necessarily from the fight, from the struggle between the many conservatives and the few revolutionaries. Hegel called for dialectics and Marx counseled revolution; Thoreau called for the study of Nature and counseled self-knowledge: every revolutionary is wild.

Therefore, in society, inside individuals and in literature as well, according to Thoreau, there are many forms and shapes to wildness. Wild Nature is simply the original, most obvious and widespread type of wilderness. Nature is so discretely fundamental that it is She that sustains towns, cities and empires; Greece, Rome and Britain are examples both of the rise and collapse of empires when Nature is exhausted: "The civilized nations—Greece, Rome, England—have been sustained by the primitive forests which anciently rotted where they stand. They survived as long as the soil is not exhausted."[53] The exhaustion being not only of the terrain, but the progressive drying up of the wild sap in all those instances, physical and spiritual. Standing as we do at the doors of environmental collapse, if the current trend of Nature's exploitation continues, Thoreau's words seem to be prescient to the fact that our current ecological era, appropriately and somberly called Anthropocene, may mark the simultaneous collective collapse of human cultures that are unable to preserve a healthy environmental equilibrium: local and relatively isolated cultures like the ones on Easter Island and in Central America are examples that come to mind. The current threat, we know, is global. That is because it is Nature that dialectically sustains cultures and their traditional places, the *polis*, cities and towns:

> "A town is saved, not more by the righteous men in it than by the woods and swamps that surround it. A township where one primitive forest waves above, while another primitive forest rots below,—such a town is fitted to raise not only corn and potatoes, but poets and philosophers for the coming age. In such soil grew Homer and Confucius and the rest, and out of such wilderness comes the Reformer eating locusts and wild honey."[54]

It is Wild Nature that sustains and feeds physically and spiritually every culture. The idea of a superposition of "forests," or "wilderness" and "a towship"—where the "natural" is situated under the "cultural"—is tantalizing; the first one at the root, the radicle, the basis of the latter, nurtured by it is fascinating in its pictorial contrasting tension and interdependence. Caring for Nature thus, becomes an essential political prerequisite both in terms of its own material sustainability as well as the necessary source of cultural and spiritual renewal. It is, thus, the necessary "infrastructure" over which the "sociopolitical culture" superstructure may flourish, if orthodox Marxists will allow the benign use of the image. Only the fertilizing powers of Nature, of wilderness Herself, may gestate creativity in society, politically, artistically and spiritually. The advent of Homer and Confucius, the poet and the sage therefore, becomes as natural as a flower or any crop. The idea of "The Reformer," a clearly biblical and messianic picture of renewal and purification of cultures and societies by "the Pure" that comes from the wilderness, untouched by civilization's corruption, John the Baptist eating locusts and wild honey and Jesus, who lived in the desert wilderness being the obvious inspirations. The tragic end of their ministry, alas, casting a dark shadow on the results of the impact of the wild on a sclerotic society. True Culture is natural, and true Nature must be embraced by Culture. In the wildernesses of the woods and imagination lies the interdependent key. Conservation of wilderness(es), thus, is extraordinarily important in a number of ways and is to be considered, consequently, as expedient and pragmatic policy: "I think each town should have a park, or rather, a primitive forest . . . where a stick should never be cut for fuel—nor for the navy, nor to make wagons, but stand and decay for higher uses—a common possession forever, for instruction and recreation."[55] The wonderfully pregnant idea of institutional National and Local parks is launched here, but the idea is not new: in Greece and Rome innumerable woods were exclusive sanctuaries dedicated to a specific Goddess/God and absolutely no economic activity whatsoever was allowed within its sacred perimeter, with the exception of fetching water, wood and flowers for the temples of the Divines. The need to preserve the wilderness as a Common, that is, as communal in its social communitarian aspect, is as amazing as the implied reference to the ontological common wilderness to which we all belong together as individuals operating interdependently in Her sacred web, to recall Marcus Aurelius. It is also remarkable to observe the subtlety of "to decay for higher uses." The explicit oxymoronic chiaroscuro beautifully conveying the idea that decay instructs and recreates is as extravagant as subtle: decay, fall and re-creation; not only playfulness but learning Nature's most important message—renewal, the recipe for wellness.

> "Live in each season as it passes; breath the air, drink the drink, taste the fruit and resign yourself to the influences of each. Let these be your only diet-drink and botanical medicines . . . [;] open all your pores and bathe in all the tides of nature, in all her streams and oceans, at all seasons. Miasma and infection are from within, not without . . . [G]row green with spring—yellow and ripe with autumn . . . [,] for all nature is doing her best each moment to make us well. She exists for no other end. Do not resist her . . . [;]nature is but another name for health."[56]

In a certain sense the best image for Thoreau's Nature is renewal. The whole of his writings may be read in that sepia light: *A Week on the Concord and Merrimack Rivers, Walden,* his essays and maybe principally his *Journal* can be seen as a recurrent ode to Nature's perennial regenerative powers. Physically, politically, intellectually and spiritually, Nature is continuously teaching us about reformation, renewal, renovation: re-creation: "All men are partially buried in the grave of custom, and of some we see only the crown of the head above ground. Better are the physically dead, for they more lively rot. Even virtue is no longer such if it be stagnant. A man's life should be constantly as fresh as this river. It should be the same channel, but a new water every instant."[57]

To follow Nature means to be willing to embrace the chaotic and regular cycle of creation and destruction: chaotic because to the individual, microscopically, sudden change may come unexpectedly; regular because the round of the seasons teach us that day follows night; summer, winter; and life, death. To able to accept and harmonize with change, to renew oneself and, in the process, renew society; this effort, this sustained tension in the quest of individual spiritual freedom and its social corollary, political liberty; this pregnant dawn of infinite promises culminates in one experience, and it is high time we experience it ourselves: awakening.

NOTES

1. Thoreau, H. D. *Journal*. In: Witherell, E. H.; Howarth, W. L.; Sattelmeyer, R.; Blanding, T. (Eds.). *The Writings Of Henry D. Thoreau*. Princeton: Princeton University Press, 1981. V.I., p. 79.

2. *Idem*, p. 168 = The Service, in Thoreau, H. D. *Collected Essays And Poems*. The Library Of America, Vol. 124. New York: The Library Of America, 2001, p.12.

3. *Journal I*, p. 203.

4. *Idem*, vol. X, pp. 251–52 pro fate; for a mixed bag, the first pages of *Walden*.

5. *Ibidem*, pp. 404–5.

6. *Ibidem, op. cit.*

7. *Ibidem*, vol. I, p. 191.

8. *Cf.* Thoreau's analysis of Emerson's poem "Sphynx." *Journal*, vol. I, p. 75.

9. *Kata physin*.

10. *To homologoumenon têi physei zên*. "to lead one's life according to Nature." Zeno, according to Diogenes Laertius, VII, 87. Diogenes Laertius. *Lives Of Eminent Philosophers*, Vol. II. Loeb Classical Library. Cambridge: Harvard University Press, 1995.

11. According to the Stoics, specifically, Nature, Zeus, Fate and Reason are synonyms. *Idem*

12. *Walking, CEP*, p. 240.

13. *Journal*, vol. I, p. 192. (= *Walking, CEP*, 247).

14. Thoreau, H. D. *Journal*. In: Sattelmeyer, R. (Ed.). *The Writings Of Henry D. Thoureau*. Princeton: Princeton University Press, 1984. V.II., P.170.

15. *Walking, CEP*, p. 251.

16. *Journal*, vol. II, p. 55.
17. Cf. Cicero, *De Natura Deorum*.
18. *Journal*, vol. II, p. 97. (= Walking, *CEP*, p. 244). Thoreau as a reader is still a desideratum.
19. *Walking, CEP*, p. 245.
20. *Journal*, vol. I, p. 284; Homer. Ossian. Chaucer., *CEP*, pp.138–40; *Walden, passim*.
21. *Journal*, vol. I, p. 471.
22. *Walking, CEP*, p. 248.
23. *Idem*, p. 251.
24. *A Week* Thoreau, H. D. *A Week On The Concord And Merrimack Rivers*. Princeton: Princeton University Press, 1980, p. 307.
25. *Journal*, vol. II, p. 457.
26. *Idem*, p. 171.
27. *Walking, CEP*, p. 246.
28. *Journal*, vol. II, p. 210.
29. *Idem*, vol. I, p. 361.
30. *Ibidem*, p. 362.
31. Thoreau, H. D. *The Journal Of H. D. Thoreau In Fourteen Volumes Bound As Two*. New York: Dover, 1962, vol. X, p. 252.
32. *Journal*, vol. I, p. 281.
33. *Journal*, vol. II, p. 193.
34. *Ibidem*, p. 470.
35. *Walden*, p. 111.
36. *Journal*, vol. I, p.80.
37. *Idem*, vol. XI, p. 285.
38. *Ibidem*, vol. II, p. 469.
39. *Ibidem*, pp. 314–15.
40. "*Direct your eyesight inward, and you will find*
    A thousand regions of your mind
    Yet undiscovered. Travel them up, and be
    Expert in home-cosmography." *Walden*, p. 320.
41. *Walden*, p. 322.
42. *A Walk to Wachusett, CEP*, p. 44.
43. Fragment 101, Diels-Kranz, *in* Freeman, Kathleen. *Ancilla to the Pre-socratic philosophers*. Cambridge, Massachusetts: Harvard University Press, 1996.
44. Fragment 116, Diels-Kranz. *Idem*.
45. Fragment 45, Diels-Kranz. *Ibidem*.
46. *Journal*, vol. IV, p. 258.
47. *Walden*, p. 133.
48. *Idem*, p. 135.
49. *Civil Disobedience, CEP*, p. 206.
50. *Idem*, p. 213.
51. Commenting on Massachusetts militiamen: "*Is this what all these soldiers, all this* training *has been for these seventy-nine years past? Have they been trained*

merely to rob Mexico, and carry black fugitive slaves to their masters?" Slavery in Massachusetts, *CEP,* p. 336.

52. There is a fertile ongoing debate as to the use of justified violence in Thoreau, as Prof. Anita Patterson kindly pointed out to me in a personal communication.

53. *Walking, CEP,* p. 243.

54. *Idem,* p. 242.

55. *Huckleberries, CEP,* p. 500.

56. *Idem,* p. 501.

57. *A week,* p. 132.

Chapter 5

Being Nature
The Inconceivable Non-Dual Experience

"There was the eye and the sun from the first."[1] Thoreau's luminous fragment of cosmogony unveils the most archaic elements which Nature gestates inside Her womb, still warm and fresh, enveloping in its placenta the All: the gaze and the light. Indeed, what else is necessary? Everything is there, the Whole is contained therein. Everything else is unfolding. Everything else is a myth. Everything else is revelation, an ancient oracle interpreted by countless seers and poets that sing its infinite variations as myriad universes dance on that single ray of light that connects the vertex of the eye and the disclosing sun. The non-duality of subject and object is already there; the complementary tension is *ab ovo*. The searching eye flirts with the sun, itself the eye of the world, both throbbing in unison. Then, the eye looks to the Other as mirror: self-consciousness arises. The look wants to know, the sun, to reveal. Eye and sun shining, everything else shines after them: appearance, wonder, ecstasy. No *Fiat Lux!* there, neither creator nor creature, only self-creation (*autopoiesis*) being, since always; both eye and sun coeval: one cannot exist without the other. Both are the unique conditions of possibility for everything else to occur, to shine, to erupt, to appear; that is, to be known as existing as such; after that, this infinite tale out of light and consciousness begins; the eye coupling with light, spawning dawn and morning, external and internal ones: enlightenments. But the perceived distance of the eye from the sun, however, also suggests the budding of a longing. It already spells a distancing which must be bridged by a return to the common source. The anamnetic process ought to reach the ultimate source, the utmost simplicity; the eye and the light are one and the result can only be an image, the very first one-Nature; Nature looking inside Herself, Her eye meeting Her sun. That first look is innocent, fresh, wild; beyond that primeval rendezvous lies only what cannot be told, what must be silenced upon: the mystery, the infinite and amorphous becoming, that ultimate untamable cosmic wilderness, whose supposed shaping and reducing to the categories of our understanding is one of our ultimate self-delusions. The marriage of the eye and the sun hides, thus, also a buried promise to be genealogically unearthed, a promise of awakening: "If you let a single ray of light through the shutter, it will go on diffusing itself without limit till it enlightens the world."[2] Thoreau is on the verge of releasing that ray of light, and we are about to be enlightened by it.

Enlightenment, awakening; as we have already seen, together with "dawn," "morning," "childhood," "youth," "music," "Spring," and "Greece," those are some of Thoreau's very particular soteriological thesaurus, his favorite code words for an inconceivable experience that lies at the very heart of his pedagogic process: "I do not propose to write an ode to dejection, but to brag as lustly as chanticleer in the morning, standing on his roost, if only to wake my neighbors up."[3] Thoreau leaves no doubt at all as to his project: awakening us; he is the crowing chanticleer and we are the anesthetized sleeping ones. But every sleeper must awake sometime, the method has already been shown—the pedagogy of the wild, attention and intimacy with Nature. Now, it is incumbent on him to describe the experience of awakening for, how could us, wretched sleepwalkers, find it, or worse, recognize it, deep in our sleep? Thoreau will describe it as well; however, he shall do so using a very special vocabulary and grammar, a wild one, a "'gramatica parda,' 'tawny grammar,' 'to express this wild and dusky knowledge.'"[4] Thus, we must be alert how to read the signs, to decipher those hieroglyphs of light: the chanticleer will crow, and those who are destined to hear and heed shall awake too.

Recalling his idyllic sojourn at Walden, Thoreau describes his sacramental practices:[5]

> "Every morning was a cheerful invitation to make my life of equal simplicity, and I may say innocence, with nature herself. I have been as sincere a worshipper of Aurora as the Greeks. I got up early and bathed in the pond; that was religious exercise, and one of the best things which I did. They say that characters were engraved on the bathing tube of king Tching-thang to this effect: 'Renew thyself completely each day; do it again, and again, and forever again.' I can understand that."[6]

I guess we all can. Morning, simplicity, innocence, Nature, Aurora (Dawn), Greece, purification. The passage powerfully displays the engorged udder from which flows the milk of renewal, Thoreau's main spiritual delicacy. Along his considerably larger and more sublime bathing tube, Walden Pond, were also engraved Spring's cryptic thawing hieroglyphs that Thoreau was able to read before they melted away on earth; they all spoke of cycle, renewal: regeneration. Nature's infinite cycles, micro and macroscopic, are segmentations of horizons of events whose interconnectedness escapes us, but Thoreau's emphasis on attention seems to prepare us, ideally, to the potential fertile and subtle decoding of the encounter of the "eye and the sun," of ourselves with everything else; in fact that encounter hides two possibilities, a perpetual forking of the path: alertness and renewal or distraction and sclerosis: either life or death, memory or oblivion, ascending or descending, light or darkness:

> "the morning, which is the most memorable season of the day, is the awakening hour. Then there is least somnolence in us; and for an hour, at least, some part of us awakes which slumbers all the rest of the day and night . . . [T]hat man that who does not believe that each day contains an earlier, more sacred and auroreal hour than he has yet profaned, has despaired of life, and is pursuing a descending and darkening way."[7]

The undiluted cosmic and epistemological Manichaeism presents us, once again, with the necessary complementariness of polarities. The descending path of oblivion and darkness, which most of us unhappily pursue, coagulates as reified spiritual, social, political and economic truths which congregate the adherents of "cattlelicism" in the domesticated environments of inauthentic and insincere existence. Contrariwise, those who are able to accord to Nature follow a different pathway:

> "all poets and heroes, like Memnon, are the children of Aurora, and emit their music at sunrise. To him whose elastic and vigorous keeps pace with the sun, the day is a perpetual morning . . . [M]orning is when I am awake and there is a dawn in me. Moral reform is the effort to throw off sleep . . . [T]he millions are awake enough for physical labor; but only one in a million is awake enough for effective intellectual exertion, only one in a hundred millions to a poetic or divine life. To be awake is to be alive."

Child of the Dawn: what a beautiful and precise monicker for Thoreau and all of his brothers and sisters who hike the same pathway of light. But then, aren't all children "children of Aurora"? Aren't all of them promises pregnant of tomorrow? Isn't every child a gamble against darkness: a new light, a new beginning? As a worshiper of the Dawn as well, Thoreau affiliates himself to the Orphics whose adherents, repeating Orpheus' original practice, woke up early and headed to the summits of the mountains to worship the first rays of the sun: renewal, purification "by the Dawn's early light" and promise in a single gesture. One of the many Orphic cosmogonies begins with the Night, and from Her comes Phanes, the golden Egg of light, which will subsequently become split as Heaven and Earth.[8] Infallibly, every day, those first rays of the rising *Sol invictus* in the Eastern horizon dispel darkness and bring with them the promise of "purification, renewal and awakening," as the ancient Romans also believed, and those three revelations, at the same time practices and results, might stand for Thoreau's motto as well. But to be awake among the sleepers is an awkward and solitary position. He necessarily had to look for awakened company elsewhere, in the past, since his contemporaries were, well . . . deeply asleep. "To be awake is to be alive. I have never yet met a man who was quite awake. How could I have looked him in the face?"[9] Alas, Thoreau never met a Buddha (an "awakened one" from Sanskrit root *BUDDH*, "to awake"), although he once reclaimed the Buddha for himself.[10] Had he met one, maybe he could have had the confirmation of his own awakening, since it takes an awakened to recognize another one. That momentous cosmic event, the meeting of Buddhas might be the one chance to understand why the infinite causal plait creates billions of lethargic zombies like us and very few awakened like them. Maybe, who knows, in the economy of the whole, we, the sleepwalkers, are as necessary as the Buddhas, after all, the only absolute precondition for awakening to happen is, first, to be asleep; or perhaps, like Jack Kerouac—another Massachusetts *poet-bodhisattva*—who once saw in his beloved seclusion atop Desolation Peak, high on the Washington Cascades: we are all destined to become Buddhas one day.[11] Well, Buddhas, as we all know, are very special, attentive beings. They are always near and aware of the processes and powers which fashions beings and events, their etiological sensibility being legendary, as Thoreau affirms when he discusses the process of illumination: "Any prospect of awakening . . . makes indifferent all times and places . . . nearest to all things is that power which fashions their being. Next to us the grandest laws are continually being executed."[12] Be it in Bodh Gaya or at Walden Pond, the same undercurrent of potential illumination is flowing. It is only a matter of tuning consciousness and light: the "*eye and the sun*"; again, we are talking about a pedagogy of the look. Sounds easy, doesn't it? Well, it isn't. Like every single Buddha from East and West taught, it is a matter of looking inside ourselves to discover the Whole, as Henry sings in one of his most beautiful and revealing poems, symptomatically named *Inward morning*.

Packed in my mind lie all the clothes
Which outward nature wears,
And in its fashion's hourly change
It all things else repairs

My eyes look inward, not without
And I but hear myself,
And this new wealth which I have got

Is part of my own self[13]

In vain I look for change abroad
And some can no difference find,
Till some new ray of peace uncalled
Illumines my inmost mind

What is it gilds the trees and clouds,
And paints the heaven so gay,
But yonder fast-abiding light
With its unchanging ray

I've heard within my soul
Such cheerful morning news,
In the horizon of my mind
Have seen such orient hues,

As in the twilight of the dawn
When the first birds awake,
Are heard within some silent wood,
Where they the small twig break,

Or in the eastern skies are seen,
Before the sun appears,
The harbingers of summer heats
Which from afar he bears[14]

The eye and the sun; the look and the light: enlightenment, awakening. We keep returning to and revolving around them as Buddhist pilgrims around their shrines, as the *wheel of saṁsāra* itself keeps revolving around unending and unsatisfied desires. Thoreau can only speak for Nature, wild Nature as we saw in his passionate words in *Walking*, because he *is* Nature: *She is his true Self*—perhaps ours as well? Describing his "*Inward morning*," his serene and silent illumination, if we hear close and attentively enough, though, we shall also be able to listen to Nature singing Herself, Thoreau being reduced—or expanded—to Her medium, Her instrument, Her flute: emptied of himself, Nature plays through him a song of awakening . . . Like his own flute, engraved by himself, that now lies sad, lonely and mute at the Concord Museum, Nature Herself carved him out of Her as a flute, a docile and faithful instrument lying on Her berry lips. The song She plays is enchanting, bewildering: the totality of the Whole is within us; we as Nature conscious of Herself, Thoreau as Nature's flute, playing his flute for Nature and, with his/Her song, awakening us in the process. This double interiority is very important. Nature is never "out there": we are always inside Her, our subjectivity being a second interiority. We are always inside Nature because we *are* Nature, Her conscious filaments, as Thoreau is never tired of pointing out to us, like a myriad of other beings whose voices we cannot hear because we are not prepared to do so. If Krishna played his flute in the woods of Vrindavana, under the moonlight by the dark and fast flowing Yamuna bewitching the *gopis*, the cowgirls, Thoreau played his flute by Walden Pond, bewitching its fishes, as a nineteenth century version of Saint Anthony's "sermon to the fishes." Like they say in India: "you cannot see Krishna, but you can hear his flute." The call is always there. Maybe we cannot hear Thoreau's flute, but we can always see who is playing through him.

Returning to the poem, there, the equivalence of internal and external is underlined as the different sides of Nature's garments. His mind "packed clothes," the structure of his understanding that limits and shapes the brief infinity of external Nature corresponds with; the sympathy of within and without, the nexus of light and change leads to awakening: the light dawns, finally; the promise is fulfilled: "We will have a dawn, and noon and serene sunset in ourselves."[15] External Nature is internalized or, conversely, internal Nature is externalized, transforming Thoreau is a diaphanous membrane that filters and reflects what originally has no precise place at all. As a crystal prism, Thoreau captures and redirects the whole gamut of colors and shapes that lie outside, reaffirming the cosmogonic principle—and metaphor—of the eye and the sun, look and light. Fundamentally, what seems to be implicated inside of him is the explicated nature of Nature as light; only light knowing Herself. The whole palette of lights and shadows dances before and inside our eyes. An eerie and serene translucent glow irradiates from nowhere and engulfs us in an iridescent kaleidoscope of diaphanous hues of consciousness that reflect and mirror the infinite variations of the luminous non-dualistic embrace of the eye and the sun. Horizons fuse and collapse as multiple Northern Lights rise and bend within us: *Aurora borealis* ignites the light from the East, slowly climbing over night's dark blue and starry dress, spreading "Dawn's rosy fingers," if I am allowed to be Homeric here; or as Thoreau enigmatically puts it: "*ex Oriente lux, ex Occidente frux*"[16]—"From the East, light; from the West, fruit"; one wonders what the "Western fruit" might be . . . "How strangely sounds of revelry strike the ear from over the cultivated fields by the wood side, while the sun is declining in the west. It is a world we had not known before. We listen and are capable of no mean act or thought. We tread on Olympus and participate in the councils of the Gods."[17] From dawn to dusk, from East to West the pathway of the sun marks the semicircle of ecstatic awareness that burns his soul. His clairaudience appears to be light related as well, the setting sun triggering a panaesthetic response from his sensibility. Moreover, either as an Eastern serene awakening or an Olympian *enthusiasm* (from Greek *en* + *theos* + *ousia*: "possessed by a God," "having a god inside"), Thoreau can savor the different available ecstasies in the divine menu of existence; further, from Buddhas' Eastern light to Greek's Olympian clarity, Thoreau's paresthesia becomes panaesthesia as his apotheosis turns light into music:

> "Sometimes we are clarified and calmed healthly as we never were before in our lives, not by an opiate, but by some unconscious obedience to the all-just laws, so that we become like a still lake of purest crystal and without effort our depths are revealed to ourselves. All the world goes by us and is reflected in our deeps. Such clarity! Obtained by such pure means! . . . [we] live and rejoice. I awoke into a music which no one about me heard . . . I feel my Maker blessing. To the sane man the world is a musical instrument. The very touch affords exquisite pleasures."[18]

Clarified, calmed, lake of crystal, our depths revealed to ourselves, reflected in the deeps, clarity, purity, joy, music, blessing, instrument: Thoreau will exhaust his vocabulary and I mine before we can describe what is going on here. Music and light comingle: his mirror-like soul becomes a crystalline pond of light, a microcosmic Walden,[19] and music, Thoreau's closest experience to the divine, as we shall soon see—or listen—becomes the voice of the enlightened one. The awakened become instruments: harps and flutes played by Nature's hands and lips of light. His particular music has a lot to do with Pythagoras' music of the spheres.[20]

> "After a still winter night I awoke with the impression that some question has been put to me, which I had been endeavoring in vain to answer in my sleep, as what-how-when-where . . . but there was dawning Nature, in whom all creatures live, looking at my broad windows with serene and satisfied face . . . I awoke to an answered question, to Nature and daylight . . . then to morning work. First I take an axe and pail and go in search of water."[21]

Like the proverbial Zen enlightening/enlightened routine—both are the same—of cutting wood and carrying water, Thoreau's morning, enlightened work, starts well before picking his axe and pail. How to answer an unasked question? The koan-nature unasked question gets an unanswered response by Nature and light-*satori*; the passage is redolent of those Zen passages where brooks and mountains sing the praise of awakening. The needless and futile unenlightened questions posed by us and addressed to us in our vain chattering during the long night of the soul—that is, our whole life long: who, when, what etc., are naturally answered by Nature and light: from foolish questions that stem from our interior darkness to the luminous answers of an enlightened Nature: which better *roshi* to have a *mondo* with? After the masterful answer, the silent and lucid clarity that flourishes from the blurred interstices of our non-duality with Nature emerge as practice: cut wood, carry water; authorless actions that sing the mantra of every Buddha: "simplicity, simplicity, simplicity."[22] Simply like that. To celebrate the event, a Zen-like poem by Thoreau:

I arose before light
To work with all my might
With my arms braced for toil
Which no obstacle can foil[23]

Steeped in light—that seems to be Thoreau's outer language garment to point to the result of his specific anamnetic process. However, he sometimes despairs of the absence of that liquid fire running through his veins. The longing stemming from the long nights of the soul exasperates him: to suffer from the valleys after experiencing the peaks depresses him . . . Nature and dawn, the eye and the sun, though, are still the basic motives when he is able to experience that ecstatic enlightenment, as in his *Stanzas*:

Nature doth have her dawn each day,
But mine are far between;
Content, I cry, for sooth to say,
Mine brightest are, I ween.

For when my sun doth deign to rise,
Though it be her noontide,
Her fairest field in shadows lies,
Nor can my light abide.

Sometimes I bask me in her day,
Conversing with my mate;
But if we interchange one ray,
Fortwith her heats abate.

Through his discourse I climb and see,
As from some eastern hill,
A brighter morrow rise to me
Than lieth in her skill.

As 't were two summer days in one,
Two Sundays come together,

Our rays united make one Sun,
With fairest summer weather.[24]

    Poetry, we remember, is the sacred language *per se* according to Thoreau; together with music, they are the only media capable of speaking of the unspeakable, of pointing out what no one, including the poet, can see: the poet can only, literally, divine. Although I am not a specialist, I believe Thoreau's poetry is unduly maligned;[25] it strikes me as a powerful instrument to express his most intimate epiphanic moments in a particularly rich naturalistic vein. Yes, he is neither a Hölderlin nor a Wordsworth, yet I believe his poetry has a very distinct and pungent flavor of wet earth and rugged beauty that, even if does not have the fluid mesmerizing music of those two Nature-singing masters, it serves him perfectly well in describing Nature as a conscious ocean of light. For instance, in one of his most intriguing poems, the itinerary is mapped out in detail and the end of the journey in the quest of awakening is clearly spelled:

I'm guided in the darkest night
By flashes of auroral light
Which over dart thy eastern home
And teach me not in vain to roam.
Thy steady light on t'other side
Pales the sunset, makes day abide,
And after sunrise stays the dawn,
Forerunner of a brighter morn.
There is no being here to me
But staying here to be
When others laugh I am not glad,
When others cry I am not sad,
But be they grieved or be they merry
I'm supernumerary.
I am a miser without blame
Am conscience stricken without shame.
An idler am I without leisure.
A busy body without pleasure
I did not think so bright a day
Would issue in so dark a night.
I did not think such sober play
Would leave me in so sad a plight,
And I should be more sorely spent
Where first I was most innocent
I thought of loving all beside

To prove to you my love was wide,
And by the rites I soared above
To show my peculiar love[26]

Among others, Chan/Taoist hermit-poet Han-Shan (Cold Mountain)[27] comes to mind as an apt parallel to Thoreau's enlightenment songs, since both poets—and many others who sang enlightenment—reveal a universe where light and darkness, pain and joy, depression and elation and every other punctuated dichotomy is solved in a narratological non-dual continuum that eclipses the apparent contradictions in a larger perspective or, as Rudolf Otto said: the *coincidentia oppositorum* ("coincidence of opposites") reveals the true nature of the *mysterium tremendum et fascinans* ("tremendous and fascinating mystery"). Besides that, both Thoreau and Han Shan in-corporate and actually become Nature: Thoreau, Walden; and Han Shan, Cold Mountain. Again, a sepia chiaroscuro technique is particularly efficient in blurring the perceived polarities into a dynamic counterpoint of discontinuous strata of light and sound. Such an aesthetic poly-phonic/ophtalmic shuffling of data registers disconcerts those who try to approach those singers with a preconceived set of principles derived from reified substantive and autonomous individualities: in Han-Shan case, insubstantial (*anātman*) non-duality and in Thoreau's substantial interdependence help to collapse the imaginary reified rigid borders between beings and phenomena.

Light, however, is far from being the only literary trope that exhausts Thoreau's extensive epiphanic vocabulary; expressions like "childhood," "youth," "music," "Spring" and "Greece," which we have already come across and, as we shall soon see again, are different images that characterize the vigor of proximity, closeness, nearness to that original, archaic spring of beauty, power and revelation. Those terms enshroud the fountain that irrigate Thoreau's texts with a fluid tenderness, a soft plasticity that accounts for the flexible force that permeates his vision of optimal relationship with Nature: "Children, who play life, discern its true law and relations more clearly than man, who fail to live it worthily, but who think that they were wiser by experience, that is, by failure."[28] Experience, we saw earlier, is completely dispensable towards happiness, both the socially inherited type as well as the individual experience of one's life. Experience is a beam that lights the rear, illuminates in hindsight, and since life is a continuous experiment there can be no recipe for either enlightenment or serenity. Children, however, adopt an unconscious ludicrous seriousness to approach life that transforms existence into a game. A very serious one at that, as anybody who has watched children at play is familiar with. This playful seriousness mixed with the absolute novelty that transforms every single experience in a uniquely virgin happening, puts them in touch with that subjective radicle at the heart of each and every perceived phenomenon. Innocence of the look is openness: "I cannot count one. I know not the first letter of the alphabet. I have always been regretting that I was not as wise as the day I was born."[29] Lost innocence is a terrible thing. It corrupts our view in as much as we cannot approach things in that ideal openness, always looking at things sideways. It also desecrates life's intrinsic sacredness in an-aesthetic and mechanical repetitions. It might be the case of ascribing to Thoreau an aesthetical justification to life, had not he himself alluded to something intangible even by art, or better still, somewhere art itself cannot reach, only point out to. I believe one of the most memorable entries of his *Journal* and a fundamental key to understand much of Thoreau's life and mission is an emotional, Wordsworthian rendering of his ecstatic experience as a child that deserves to be quoted in full:

"Methinks my present experience is nothing; my past experience is all in all. I think that no experience which I have today comes up to or is comparable with the experiences of my boyhood—and not only this is true—but as far back as I can remember I have unconsciously referred to a previous state of existence. 'For life is a forgetting,' etc. Formerly methought nature developed as I developed and grew up with me. My life was ecstasy. In youth, before I lost any of my senses, I can remember that I was all alive, and inhabited my body with inexpressible satisfaction, both its weariness and its refreshment were sweet to me. This earth was the most glorious musical instrument, and I was audience to its strains. To have such sweet impressions made on us, such ecstasies begotten of the breezes! I can remember how I was astonished. I said to myself,—I said to others—'There comes into my mind or soul an indescribable infinite all absorbing divine heavenly pleasure, a sense of elevation and expansion, and I have had nought to do with it. I perceive that I am dealt with by superior powers This is a pleasure, a joy, an existence which I have not procured myself—I speak as a witness on the stand and tell what I have perceived.' The morning and the evening were sweet to me, and I lead a life aloof from society of men. I wondered if a mortal had ever known what I knew. I looked in books for some recognition of a kindred experience but, strange to say, I found none. Indeed I was slow to discover that other men had had this experience, for it had been possible to read books and to associate with men on other grounds. The maker of me was improving me. When I detected this interference I was profoundly moved. For years I marched as to a music in comparison with which the military music of the streets is noise and discord. I was daily intoxicated and yet no man could call me intemperate. With all your science can you tell how it is, and whence it is, that light comes into the soul?"[30]

I wonder if either in Eastern or Western lay literature such an extraordinary description of an ecstatic testimony is to be found. It is not only emotionally pungent and astonishingly rich in any whatsoever way one cares to look at it; it is also unbelievably painful and impossible not to sympathize with someone who knew and fell from such an exalted state. I would like to proceed slowly here, since we are approaching the region of delicacies.

Whenever I read that passage I like to imagine Thoreau as a four-year-old kid, holding his mother hand and walking through Walden Woods enveloped in light, one of the first experiences in his life he can recall.[31] It is impossible not to relate the sheer magic of his remembrance with the echo of one of William Wordsworth masterpieces, *Odes on Intimations of Immortality from Recollections of Early Childhood*:

There was a time when meadow, grove and stream,
The earth and every common sight
To me did seem
Apparelled in celestial light . . .[32]

The Wordsworthian tint almost carries us away and disguises a very important allusion to "previous states of existence." That is intriguing. Thoreau's reticence about reincarnation notwithstanding, his chain of "remembrance"—even from previews existences—seems to confirm the importance of the anamnetic process towards the archaic kernel, the hardcore of existence, for "life is forgetting etc," or, in Wordsworth's words: "our birth is but a sleep and a forgetting. . . ." If life is sleep and forgetting, remembering allows us to retrieve, at least in the realm of an incandescent pedagogical anamnetic memory, the lost magic glow that envelops the world from a childish look. Again, the look and the light mark the experience of non-dual singularity: a culminating vortex of light and beauty, whose intersecting rays condense as silent wonder. A sensual overflowing of luminosity both from inside and outside that ignites his senses to such an extent that they were burnt. Thoreau's literal sensual ecstatic burnout serves as an apt metaphor to suggest his life work might also be considered as an attempt to reenact the conditions of possibility towards the lost ecstatic existence of his early childhood. In a certain sense we could understand all of his ulterior works as a huge Proustian memoir that ideally might recreate an "instasy," an internal simulacrum of ecstasy, as the actual reality seems to rob him of the experiencing of its past deeply felt magic. His childhood had, thus, the distinctive and unique miracle of recurrent epiphanic moments, as he recalls somewhere else: "My imagination, my sense of the miraculous, is not so excited by any event as by the remembrance of my youth."[33] Such a blessed childhood, bathed continuously in a halo of ecstatic light may have helped him to develop his belief that "every child begins the world again, to some extent,"[34] his internal child, like his internal savage—if both are not the same, seems to be redirecting him continuously to that genealogical fountain of sacredness. Such a unique experience, unshared by none of his acquaintances, appears to have isolated him even more in his secluded and solitary innocent and incomprehensible quizzical halo of light that gently envelops his nature: religious people would gladly die for a fraction of that shroud of luminous wonder, in his case, though, the obvious gratuity of the phenomenon, described as objectively as possible, paired with the marionette-like sensation, creates an environment of inevitability that adds a precious luster to the intoxication from gyrating in a whirlwind of earthen and breezes begotten magic. Winged by heavenly pleasures, the elevation and expansion inflate his detached testimony so that the epiphanic ardor becomes infectious and an unavoidable dizziness makes it impossible to locate its source. Lastly, the skepticism over instrumental science derides the possibility of explanation: the only alternative is retracing the steps to the beginning; the iridescent mythopoetic embryonic *in illo tempore*: the meeting of the light and the soul; an unashamed and necessary reinstatement of the original awe, the luminous wonder of mystery towards that archaic spermatic fecundation of the eye by the sun.

Corresponding to the innocence and non-dualistic marriage of the child and Nature in microscopic scale stands the macroscopic freshness of that sublime clarity of those elder children of the sun, Thoreau's brothers and sisters in the worship of light and Dawn, the Greeks: "the Greeks were boys in the sunshine."[35] More than an epochal phenomenon in human history, those halcyon days of Hellenic Mediterranean azure signify to Thoreau a spiritual attitude encapsulated in their inimitable and irresistible *paideia*, whose mix of Mythology, Art and Natural Philosophy overarches the project which was delineated at the beginning of this promenade of ours through Thoreauvian woods. Their literature, plastic monuments and Philosophy are eternal testaments to that unique ingenious attitude of spiritual and material solar equilibrium; thus, Ancient Greece is neither a place nor a time, but a certain *look*. Yes, a luminous one: "The Greeks, as the Southerns generally, expressed themselves with more facility than we in distinctly lively images . . . Aeschylus had a clear eye for the commonest things . . . [t]he Greeks were stern but simple children in their literature. We have gained nothing by the few ages which we have the start of them. This universal wondering at those old men is as if a matured grown person should discover that the aspirations of his youth argued a diviner life than the contented wisdom of his manhood."[36] The subsequent ages were not able to surpass the stupendous achievements of the Greeks: how could they? The Hellenic gaze was still virgin and their love of war—the *agon*—so familiar to Thoreau's own soul,[37] made him feel comfortable in their presence. Their ferocity towards other Greeks who shared the same language, customs and beliefs sounds incomprehensible for us, tame and late people that we are, but Thoreau detected with impressive surgical firmness the common roots of their unsurpassed philosophy, art and savagery in war: wildeness. The Greeks were still wild.

Their wildness was, to be sure, an unwanted and unforeseen inheritance. Lying at the crossroads of multiple ancient civilizations they have somehow managed to turn an unadulterated clear and sharp innocent look to the world that surrounded them. From Homer to Thales to Aeschylus and Heraclitus, Thoreau said things about the Greeks that would transform Nietzsche in a revolutionary classicist some decades after him. That, of course, does not aim at diminishing Nietzsche's extraordinary Hellenic reinterpretations of the by then widespread Winckelmann's classical representation of the Greek ideal as "noble simplicity and calm grandeur,"[38] but it is fascinating to see how an understandable but overly domesticated view of Thoreau as a pacifist and mystic only has incapacitated, so far, a better and more profound reading of Thoreau's younger years novel and subversive classicism. If it is true that Nietzsche shook the pillars of Olympus, Thoreau was already there savoring ambrosia with the Goddesses and Gods.

> "Without instituting a wider comparison I might say that in Homer there is more of the innocence and serenity of youth than in more modern and moral poets. The Iliad is not Sabbath but morning reading, and men cling to this old song, because they have still moments of unbaptized and uncommitted life which give them appetite for more. There is no cant in him, as there was no religion. We read him with a rare sense of freedom and irresponsibleness, as though we trod on native ground, and were autochthones of the soil."[39]

Only an extraordinarily acute eye could detect in the *Iliad* child-like innocence. That fierce song of anger, war, fire, iron and blood that inaugurates Western literature stands apart from everything else that came to be produced by our subsequent seers, poets and writers, according to Thoreau. For those that have understandably construed a pacifist and mystic Thoreau, it is important to underscore sharply the fact that serenity and war have to be understood in a necessary pendular diapason that integrates and transcends the divergent but complementary poles of the movements. The Greeks were serene because they were still natural in their ferocity. Such proximity to the autochthonous vigor of Nature, both in diachronic and synchronic terms, feeds the fascination they still exert on Thoreau—and us. "The morning wind forever blows, the poem of creation is uninterrupted; but few are that hear it. Olympus is but the outside of the earth everywhere."[40] Cosmogenesis is a continuous poetry in more than one sense: it is an infinite *poiesis*, literally, a "making" in Greek. It is a perpetual, unending in-making, an infinite becoming; it is Beauty fluidly crystallizing as Cosmos, the beautiful cosmic order; it is the sacred register of Poetry founding existence in all its radical vigor, as a song of Being: poetry presentifies Being, poetry is ontophanic. Alas, we sleepers are not only blind but deaf as well—and most certainly dumb too; however, some are dumb because they cannot physically say anything, most of others because they are not able to say much, but very, very few are those who become mute of wonder and awe in witnessing this on-going poetry of spectacular beauty: what could the latter possibly say? Those are the ones that live in Olympus, the radical Other-Place from our spurious presentism; Olympus is a mountain, i.e., the constant connection, a channel between and the meeting of translucent crystalline azure Sky and dark Earth of ample bosom, a world-axis of truth and beauty; but Olympus is also the home of the *theoi*, the divine immortals forever feasting to the music of Apollo and the song and dance of the muses, and music, as we saw earlier on, is an epiphanic language for Thoreau as well. We have to develop a musical *ear* if we are to understand his song of non-dual awakening; let's try to get acquainted with the language of music now before we are able to hear it.

"True words are those—transport, rapture, ravishment, ecstasy. These are the words I want. This is the effect of music. I am rapt away by it, out of myself. These are truly poetical words. I am inspired, elevated, expanded. I am on the mount."[41] Poetry is music; music is poetry. Both are the only languages as far as epiphanic experience is concerned. To be taken away implies *ex-stasis*, "to be out of one self," out of our ordinary and vulgar cacophony that arrests us to our pedestrian dimension, in contrast to the elevating powers of song and poetry; rapture implies a rupture with the meaningless and dissonant language that we, the sleepers, produce: a cacophony of isolated sclerotic voices that do not speak but creak, act and exist out-of-tune: "Some sounds seem to reverberate along the plain, and then settle to earth again like dusk; such are Noise, Discord, Jargon. But such only as spring heavenward, and I may catch from steeples and hilltops in their upward course, which are more refined parts of the former, are the true sphere of music,—pure, unmixed music,—in which no wail mingles."[42] Our language is characterized by noise and discord in contrast to the true nature of music, that is by far the best medium to describe the eruption of the divine experience, whose transcendent nature is best sung:

"in a world of peace and love music would be the universal language . . . [A]ll beings obey music as they obey virtue. It is a herald of virtue. It is God's voice . . . [T]he universe needed only to hear a divine melody, that every star might fall into its proper place . . . [I]t entails a surpassing affluence on the meanest thing; riding sublime over the heads of sages and soothing the din of philosophy."[43]

Music as a universal language presupposes a world of peace and love, implying that this old world of ours, violent and cruel, will have to make do with ordinary language, the language where silence is just an uncomfortable interstice between two noises, and not the true origin of language. Music as the "voice of God" is an appealing image if we remember that in many religious traditions, the Judean-Christian included, the creational act is carried out by God's voice. Music is way over and above the thought of the sages and the quarrelsome din of Philosophy; in fact, we are the instruments of this divine symphony: "the human soul is a silent harp in God's quire, whose strings need only be swept by the divine breath to chime in with the harmonies of creation. Every pulse-beat is in exact time with the cricket's chant."[44] This synchrony of us with Nature is the result of Divine intervention. As the Divine breaths through or thrums us, we are in symphony with the sounds of the other natural instruments: birds, winds and Thoreau's favorite Nature's singer, the crickets. The consonance of this universal choir in unison is the sound correlate of the perfection of Nature. One has only to empty oneself to become flute or stretch oneself to become string and abandon the idea of authorship: we are docile instruments in the hands or on the lips of the Cosmos. Those sounds are each creature's language in this unending symphony, or Opera, with all the drama and pathos unconsciously producing the necessary dissonances to create a most sophisticated polyphonic concerto.

Thoreau's sensibility to music infiltrates his worldview, or better, worldhearing in such a way that he seems to believe implicitly that our vain chattering obfuscates the primordial musical sound that stirs the creation, revealing a Pythagorean cosmos as a well-tuned orchestra. This orchestra, though, is not to be approached merely with our audition, on the contrary, we are to tune-in with the whole of our being:

> "Pythagoras did not procure for himself a thing of this kind trough instruments or the voice, but employing a certain ineffable divinity, and which is difficult to apprehend, he extends his ears and fixed his intellect in the sublime symphonies of the world, he alone hearing and understanding, as it appears, the universal harmony and consonance of the spheres, and the stars that are moved through them, and which produce a fuller and more intense melody than anything effected by mortal sounds."[45]

We have already had the opportunity of pointing out a Pythagorean hue in Henry's writings and thought. If we bear in mind that in ancient Greece Pythagoreanism and Orphism mixed in some cultic spaces and philosophical environments, principally in Platonism, to which Thoreau was exposed both by his and Emerson's readings and the latter writings, we can better understand some things that are being said here about music. First of all, the above quote comes from Iamblichus (fourth century), a Syrian Neoplatonist that wrote a famous biography of Pythagoras; secondly, both Thoreau and Emerson were profoundly influenced by the prolific translations of Thomas Taylor (1758–1835), a "neo-Neoplatonic" (*sic*) English writer and translator of many Pythagoric and Platonic texts, whose work was highly praised by Emerson and Thoreau. The idea of "the harmony of the spheres," an extraordinarily enchanting natural sound produced by the planets and stars in symphony as they move around the heavens is a recurrent theme whenever Thoreau writes about music. Moreover, to the Pythagoreans, music had not only a depurative and healing physical and spiritual power, but also a profound impact on our minds as well, since music is able to change our mental moods in a number of ways. Plato and music come explicitly together in a number of places[46] in Thoreau's writings, and according to him, music not only creates beauty but sustains the cosmos as well: "music is the sound of universal laws promulgated";[47] such a powerful description of music recalls the multiple coextensive manifestations of natural universal laws; thus, music is coeval with natural law in juridical terms ("Natural law" contrasted to "Statute Law," as we saw in Antigone), in science (Nature's laws' description, "*Philosophia Naturalis*"), in morality (Ethical behavior, "*What is natural?*") and, as we can see, in music as both universal language and manifestation of natural processes ("*the music of the spheres*"); moreover, and this is very interesting, music is also a perennial constitutional essence of reality that encodes a mysterious message to those who can hear and decipher it:

> "Of what manner of stuff is the web of time wove, when these consecutive sounds called a strain of music can be wafted down through the centuries from Homer to me, and Homer have been conversant with that same unfathomable mystery and charm which so newly tingles my ears? Those single strains, these melodious cadences which plainly proceed out of a very deep meaning and a sustained soul, are the interjections of God."[48]

Music can decompose Nature into Her minimal notes and life into chords, weaving Time, mystery and sound in an intricate tress of counterpoints woven by the scales of cosmic beauty. The question about the "stuff" that allows music to be transported through the web of Time is not simply a question about sound or music: it is a question about Being itself, in as much as the "web of time" must necessarily be contiguous with the very becoming of reality in a diachronic manner in order to make it possible for sound to be and be wafted along the flux of this mysterious reality; slightly rearranging the question: "what is the constitutional frame that allows the percolation of that openness towards the Mystery through Time?" That openness into the mysterious heart of reality is an instantiation of the many divine powers of music, it is an inter-jection, literally, a "throwing in between," an opening into the divine heart of Nature that is always available. It is God's or the Divine's pledge of the undying possibility of awakening itself, an assurance that along History, the unfolding story of Being being, the aesthetic ecstasy is near at hand, or near at ear, for since Homer—always him—the availability of the divine experience is close to us, if only we can, or care to listen attentively. The wafting of the message of awakening along the carvings of this Aeolian harp into which Nature breathes most mellifluously—literally "flowing with honey"—is to be decoded only by those whose ears are open to hear the extremely old and always new same song of illumination. Thoreau was such a one; a simple thrumming of a guitar is enough to the triggering of this sort of experience in him:

> "I hear one thrumming guitar below stairs. It reminds me of moments I have lived. What a comment on our life is the least strain of music! It lifts me up above all the dust and mire of the universe. I soar or hover with clean skirts over the field of my life . . . [T]he way in which I am affected by this faint thrumming advertises me that there is still some health and immortality in the springs of me . . . [I]t releases me; it bursts my bonds . . . [T]alk of infidels! Why, all of the race of man, except in the rarest moments when they are lifted above themselves by an ecstasy are infidels . . . [T]his poor, timid, unenlightened, thick-skinned creature, what can it believe? I am, of course, hopelessly ignorant and unbelieving until some divinity stirs within me. Ninety-nine one-hundredths of our lives are mere hedgers and ditchers, but from time to time we meet with reminders of our destiny. We hear the kindred vibrations, music! And we put out our dormant feelers unto the limits of the universe. We attain to a wisdom that passeth understanding. The stable continents undulate. The hard and fixed becomes fluid. When I hear music I fear no danger, I am invulnerable, I see no foe. I am related to the earliest times and the latest."[49]

The ecstatic whirlwind of music and light that elevates him to the limits of the universe depicts a classical dissolving of Time-Space structures which reveal Thoreau's non-dual contiguity with the intrinsic matrix of reality. His "relation" to the "earliest times" seems to point to his reaching the very end of the anamnetic process in terms of that archaic experience of proximity to the common origins, the kernel of himself, Nature; on the other end of the spectrum, I believe his "relation" to "the latest" times may allude to the teleological ecstatic nature of his/our existence, that is, in terms of arriving at the veritable finality of his/our life journey, the confluence of ourselves and Nature.

However, instrumental music is a necessary aesthetic trigger only for those who have a callous sensibility: "Debauched and worn-out senses require the violent vibrations of an instrument to excite them, but sound and still joyful senses, not enervated by luxury, hear music in the wind and rain and running water . . . [m]usic is perpetual, and only hearing is intermittent. I hear it in the softened air of these warm February days."[50] Nature Herself speaks continuously and Her voice is a song for those who are blessed enough to hear Her singing. Thoreau hears the purifying melodies that exude from the elements in harmony. The song of the dancing brooks against the mossy stones, the wind caressing the green canopy, the owls, crickets and frogs in their infinite opera; such an elemental symphony is a polyphonic choral of different, but not dissonant voices, arranged in euphonic notes that expose each being's singularity and reveal their innermost nature to those attentive ears that can open-up to Nature's plural voices. Such openness prepares us to further revelations, those who cannot be conveyed by ordinary words, in fact, music—and poetry—is a propedeutic initiation to the final revelation of this essay, the experience of our non-duality with Nature, and the time has come to open our ears to it.

"To be serene and successful we must be at one with the universe."[51] Serenity, calm and quiet: "*Hesychia*" in Greek. Not only a specific goal for the Pythagoreans and the Eleatic school—and to Western's philosophical tradition as a whole, but one of the most obscure Goddesses of Hellas as well. According to Pindar (VI–V b.c.e), the Theban lyric poet, She is the daughter of *Dike*, Justice.[52] In Rome She was called *Quies*, the "Quiet one" or "*Silentia*," the Silent one. It is tempting to understand "serenity," "calm" as the result of the behavior of the just person (*dikaios*), however, Thoreau leaves no doubt as to the real origin of "serenity" and "success": the experience of non-duality with the Cosmos, with the All. But are we not already "one with the universe"? Are we not already woven, inextricably imbricated into the veins and tendons of Nature? Yes . . . and no. Yes, we are Nature and no, we are not conscious of the fact. For all of those reasons we saw along this essay, we are forgetful of that. Our cosmic umbilical cord was severed by the scissors of techniques and those ideological layers of varnish that transformed us in strangers at our own home. No, we are not Nature anymore and that is the problem. We, as instruments, are out-of-tune, we have to be retuned, for our pitch is not a natural one anymore, we are hybrids that operate in varying cyclothimic frequencies whose final results are our poor lives of "quiet desperation." Our distancing, our separation begins early on:

> "In a sense the babe takes its departure from Nature as the grown man his departure out of her, and so during nonage is at one with her, and as a part of herself . . . [I]t passes through Nature to manhood and becomes unnatural, without being as yet quite supernatural . . . [H]is actions do not adorn Nature nor one another, nor does she exist in harmony but in contrast with them. She is not

their willing scenery. We conceive that if a true action were to be performed it would be assisted by Nature, and perhaps be fondled and reflected many times as the rainbow."[53]

The colors of the rainbow collect the whole gamut of the visible frequencies of light when they dance their way through the rain. The harmony of plurality in the One, "*e pluribus unum*," the intrinsic richness of the differences is squandered by the sclerotic pulling force of social mores and monies. Our familiarity with the Whole, our belonging to the All has to be retraced, recovered and retrieved. That anamnetic process, we have seen, can be modalized in different ways in diverse contexts, here, once again, childhood's innocence, that toothless wilderness—just to contrast it to the toothless sclerosis—is the arche, the lost Grail of our symbiotic interdependence with this infinite web of light whose serenity is one of the rewards, as Thoreau beautifully paints in his communion:

> "This is a delicious evening, when the whole body is one sense, and imbibes delight through every pore. I go and come with a strange liberty in Nature, a part of herself. As I walk along the stony shore of the pond in my shirt sleeves, though it is cool as well as cloudy and windy, and I see nothing special to attract me, all the elements are unusually congenial to me. The bullfrogs trump to usher in the night, and the note of the whippoorwill is borne on the rippling wind from over the water. Sympathy with the fluttering alder and poplar leaves almost takes away my breath; yet, like the lake, my serenity is rippled but not ruffled."[54]

When one's body becomes only one sense, it means that one's whole sensibility is tuned in an about-to-snap tension that necessarily deterritorializes both sense data and sense itself. One is not anymore, one ceases to be: only Nature is. As his elemental frame promenades through beauty dense of consciousness and slowly dissolves, only tenuous and diaphanous sympathetic bonds allows us to perceive the contours of sense and sense data drafting blurring fluid limits that galvanize a spiral of elements and conscious light that can only tentatively be called "Thoreau"; "His" serenity is not actually "his" anymore: how could it be? It is Nature-conscious-of-Herself that saunters inside Herself now, by the shores of Her own eye, Walden, that drop of light on Her eternal face. Delight and serenity fuse as The Maiden progress among Her creatures, other aspects of Her: the frog, the whippoorwill and that breathless and serene and smiling translucent figure once called Thoreau. No, he is not anymore:

I cannot come near to God and Heaven
Than I live to Walden even
I am its stony shore,

And the breeze that passes o'er;
In the hollow of my hand
Are its water and its sand,
And its deepest resort
Lies high in my thought.[55]

The transfiguration is complete. "He" cannot help but assume "his" old/new persona, Nature. The masks fall, the anamnetic process is over. He's back home, hugged by The Maiden . . . it is difficult to proceed here, since words become wobbly and refuse to yield sense; letters become little dancing sparkles of light: She is he/im discovering to be Her. He was always Her/She forgotten-of-Herself as him. Thoreau merges with Walden and then with the whole of Nature. Their total interpenetration transforms Thoreau's voice in Nature's stream of consciousness extrapolating throughout Her senses and looking at herself internally with Thoreau's eyes. The promise is fulfilled, non-duality: *en panta*, "everything is One," as the ancients said; the inward morning has finally dawned, serenely.

And with the dawn, we approach the end of our trail, through deep darkness, many perils and beauty, for ours was a track during the night of the soul, when our sleep is most profound. But our guide was a reliable one, wasn't he? We can still see his footprints ahead of us in the thawing clay of Spring. Yes, our guide: who is he, after all?

In one of his most intriguing poems, *Great Friend*, our guide seems to be looking at a mirror, dreaming of and looking for a man which he already is:

I walk in nature still alone
And know no one
Discern no lineament nor feature
Of any creature.
Though all the firmament
Is over me bent,
Yet still I miss the grace
Of an intelligent and kindred face.
I still must seek a friend
Who does with nature blend,
Who is the person in her mask,
He is the man I ask.
Who is the expression of her meaning,
Who is the uprightness of her leaning,
Who is the grown child of her weaning
The center of this world,
The face of nature,

The site of human life,
Some sure foundation
And nucleous of a nation-
At least a private station.
We twain would walk together
Through every weather
And see this aged nature
Go with a bending stature.[56]

Thoreau, Nature's double, looking deep inside the mirror, unveils his true face: he is the one that blends with Nature, his true and expanded Self finally recognized; he is one of the infinite masks She wears in the cosmic game of hide-and-seek. As Heraclitus reminds us, She likes to hide, and which better place to hide than inside Her creatures, Her infinite masks that unconsciously and most of time revolt against Her unalterable and incomprehensible decrees and those very few who, like sleepers, are only waiting for a Chanticleer to announce a new morning and an internal awakening? He is the Chanticleer, the one who in crowing awakens us; it is he who expresses Her meaning, for as we saw earlier on, he is not only Her first and foremost champion, but Her true voice, Her flute, hanging from Her full lips and being played by Her warm and mellifluous breath; he is the uprightness, the moral column, the vertex of Nature's Self-knowing eye; he is the grown child who knew he lost something long ago and worked so hard to retrieve it, who used to buoy in Her infinite sea of serene light; he is the center of this world, the pivot around which She gravitates in myriad forms always inviting him to know himself and study Her; he is Her face, one of Her last masks, one of Her true and innermost self-disguising doubles who is perennially willing to embark in Her wildest adventures; he is the radicle, the budding vigor of enchanting and bewildering and untamable life; he is the foundation, the dissident, for true democracy relies on dissidents and not on sleepwalking conformists; he is a deeply-set pile for the building of a true nation, a nation, many nations, of true, sincere and authentic women and men, and not a bunch of cowardly sclerotic simulacra of grotesque consumerism that bow slavishly to the State's sitting puppets of the economic, political and ideological powers that help to deform both human and Nature like a merciless predator: he is you and me; he is the wild one, the forgotten one: *Nature*. She is Henry David Thoreau.

NOTES

1. *Dark ages in* Thoreau, H. D. *Collected Essays And Poems*. The Library Of America, Vol. 124. New York: The Library Of America, 2001, p. 91. (*CEP*)

2. *The service, idem*, p. 11.
3. *Walden*, Thoreau, H. D. *Walden*, Princeton: Princeton University Press, 1971, p. 84.
4. *Walking*, *CEP*, p. 249.
5. According to Thoreau, an unspecified dictionary defines sacramental as an "outward and visible sign of an inward and spiritual grace." *Walden*, p. 69. It is important to bear in mind the correspondence between the internal and external is relevant here to fully understand the sequence of the text.
6. *Walden*, p. 88.
7. *Idem*, p. 89.
8. *Cf. Orphic Hymns, The.* Translation, Introduction And Notes By Athanassakis, A. N. And Wolkow, B. M. Baltimore: The Johns Hopkins University Press, 2013, p. 86.
9. *Walden*, p. 90.
10. *A Week*, p. 67.
11. A recurrent theme in Kerouac's *Desolation angels, Lonesome traveler* and *The Dharma bums*.
12. *Walden*, p. 134.
13. This is a variant stanza only found in *Journal*, Thoreau, H. D. *Journal*. In: Witherell, E. H.; Howarth, W. L.; Sattelmeyer, R.; Blanding, T. (Eds.). *The Writings Of Henry D. Thoreau*. Princeton: Princeton University Press, 1981. V.I., p.291.
14. *The Inward morning*, Thoreau, H. D. *A Week On The Concord And Merrimack Rivers*. Princeton: Princeton University Press, 1980, p. 294–95.
15. *Journal*, vol. I, p. 159.
16. *Walking*, *CEP*, p. 237.
17. *Journal*, vol. I, p. 55.
18. Thoreau, H. D. *Journal*. In: Sattelmeyer, R. (Ed.). *The Writings Of Henry D. Thoureau*. Princeton: Princeton University Press, 1984. V.II., p. 268–69.
19. *Cf.* Thoreau's description in *Walden*, pp. 175–77.
20. *E.g.*: *A Week*, pp. 71, 103, 132, 152, 317. Music and Pyhagoras, *A week*, p. 176. The discrete and pervasive presence of a Pythagorean vein in Thoreau's work is quite interesting and deserves further attention. See note 45, below.
21. *Walden*, p. 282.
22. *Idem*, p. 91.
23. Unnamed poem, *CEP*, p. 539.
24. *Stanzas*, *CEP*, p. 529.
25. Most scholars, unfortunately, disregard and quickly dismiss Thoreau's poetry; unnecessarily embarrassed, they generally hurry past it. Yet, it may have been wise of Thoreau to opt for a poetic prose instead of a prosaic poetry.
26. Unnamed poem, *CEP*, pp. 539–40.
27. There are excellent translations of Han-Shan in English. Gary Snider's and J.P. Seaton's are among the best.
28. *Walden*, p. 96.
29. *Idem*, p. 98.
30. *Journal*, vol. II, pp. 306–7.

31. He retells the experience in *Walden*, "Bean Fields," p. 155.
32. Wordsworth, W. *The major works*. Oxford: Oxfor World's Classics, 2011, p. 297.
33. *Journal*, vol. II, p. 33.
34. *Walden*, p. 28.
35. *Journal*, vol. I, p. 165.
36. *Idem*, vol. I., p. 116.
37. *"I have a deep sympathy with war, it so apes the gait and bearing of the soul." Journal*, vol. I, p. 136, *et al. Cf.* Nietzsche's *The Homeric agon*.
38. *"Edle Einfalt und stille Grösse."*
39. *Journal*, vol. I., p. 284.
40. *Walden*, p. 85.
41. *Journal*, Thoreau, H. D. *The Journal Of H. D. Thoreau In Fourteen Volumes Bound As Two*. New York: Dover, 1962, vol. IV, pp. 466–67.
42. *Journal*, vol. I, p. 53.
43. *The service, CEP*, p. 143.
44. *Journal*, vol. I. p. 53.
45. *Idem*, p. 142–43.
46. *The service, CEP*, p. 13.
47. *A Week*, p. 175.
48. *Journal*, vol. I, pp. 316–17.
49. *Idem*, vol. IX, pp. 217–18.
50. *Ibidem*, vol. IX, pp. 244–45.
51. *Ibidem*, vol. VI, pp. 310–11.
52. *Olympica*, IV. 18; *Pythian*, viii. 1. *Pindar's victory songs*, translated by Frank J. Nisetich. Baltimore and London: The Johns Hopkins University Press, 1980.
53. *Journal*, vol. I, p. 232.
54. *Walden*, p. 129.
55. *Idem*, p. 193.
56. *CEP*, p. 601.

Conclusion
A Footpath in the Woods

Alas, our promenade with Thoreau is over . . . but it was a nice sauntering, wasn't it, gentle reader? He, always a most peculiar man, has already dashed ahead, leaving us behind and gone home whistling to check on his friends: the frogs, breams and woodchucks, leaving us a bit lost in the middle of this footpath in the woods, and the woods may look terribly frightening to those who are not used to the groves of Pan—*panic*. Ah! But that seems to be, in fact, simply lack of familiarity with Nature. As soon as one starts to frequent Her shaded crags and bath in Her brooks and pearl white sand beaches, everything changes. She becomes the origin, the arche, the Maiden: how could She possibly wish us harm? No, our guide was right: She is always good to Her children. As Nature wanted, Thoreau is already gone, a-huckleberrying somewhere else, but if we look closer, maybe he has left a message for us written on the bark of some venerable beech tree. And maybe it is written on it: "I live in the perpetual verdure of the globe. I die in the annual decay of nature."[1]

Life and death: is not Nature precisely that, an infinite cycle of creation, destruction and recreation? Cycle inside cycle, sphere inside sphere, small apparent dots on this infinite lace of light, from subatomic particles to molecules, cells, plants, animals, planets and galaxies; always changing, flowing in this infinite holographic ballet of supreme beauty and elegance, this cosmos of ours, so magnificent and so delicate, this web of brief ecstasies available to each and everyone if one cares to look: "To the indifferent and casual observer the laws of nature are science—To the enlightened and spiritual they are morality—or modes of divine life."[2] The very same grain of sand dissolves as crystals of light in the fingers of Beauty: Nature, who is She? Who are we? To live according to Nature is more than just a high-sounding but empty word of wisdom, it is an invitation to an infinite discovery, an endless perplexity, a philosophical and poetical dance along life, punctuated by few ecstasies along a truly rough but fascinating road, if only we truly look to Nature and to ourselves as well, we, an openness to the infinite:

> "If with closed ears and eyes I consult consciousness for a moment, immediately are all walls and barriers dissipated, earth rolls from under me, and I float, by the impetus derived from the earth and the system, a subjective, heavily laden thought, in the midst of an unknown and infinite sea, or else heave and swell like a vast ocean of thought, without rock or headland, where all riddles solved, all straight lines making their two ends meet, eternity and space gamboling familiarly through my depths. I am from beginning, knowing no end, no aim. No sun illumines me, for I dissolve all lesser lights in my own intenser and steadier light. I am a restful kernel in the magazine of the universe."[3]

Thoreau clearly awakened and bequeathed to us the itinerary, the principles and practices which led to his inward morning: alas, when shall ours come? From his "methodological doubt" over his socially inherited sclerotic "wisdom" as his point of departure until the experiencing of his unity with the Whole, Thoreau's trajectory seems to point to the need of a profound, caring and sustained engagement both with our innermost selves and with Nature. Intimacy with Her laws, cycles, moods and inhabitants allows us to reinterpret ourselves and our roles in the ecological economy of the All, ideally to the point where we would be able to celebrate our non-duality with the radicle of Being, the first budding of the unsurpassed beautiful flower of self-realization. When we recognize ourselves as Nature and become able to perceive our belonging to Her in a sacred way—that delicate golden, green and blue filigree of light wrought by Necessity's hands—we may then be able to transform the most pedestrian datum of sensibility into an epiphanic moment, for to be one with Her means in fact to be really Her, to be actually conscious of being Being, a self-aware sentient mode of Hers whose imbrications and ramifications spread infinitely in space and time reorganizing and correcting our sorrowful look into a silent and serene smile that is the only and best reward to know one self and Herself as perfect; perfection in the sense that it is only possible to be what we truly are, our misadventures and shortcomings being necessary stages to realizing our potential inexorable luminous nature.

"When most at one with Nature I feel supported and propped by myriad influences."[4] The interdependence of "me" and "the other" collapses borders as we penetrate in the darkest mystery of all, contiguity being simply a misplaced look that is yet to be recalibrated by the density of the interpenetration and interaction of the continuous polycentric flux of elements, beings and phenomena that inaugurates the theurgic self-empowerment: "I am time and the world. I assert no independence. In me are summer and winter—village life and commercial routine—Pestilence and famine and refreshing breezes—joy and sadness—life & death."⁵ The myriad phenomena dance holographically on the mirrored surface of our enlightened mind; Nature knowing Herself through us; we as windows that open inwards to our depths and outwards to Her depths, both depths being exactly one and the same, only language being incapable of accounting for it. The horizon changes continuously, yet it is always in the very same place. It is the result of the meeting of the infinite of the Sky with the infinite of the Earth. The frontier, the *limines*, the limit, the fundamental and the ultimate promise: the always regenerating coming-to-be. Like truth-ultimate truth-unreachable because ever receding, intangible and inconceivable, the horizon is always where the gaze reaches, where Earth of ample bosom meets starry and rainy Sky, the hierogamic union that symbolizes our wholeness, our morning, our dawn: "Morning is when I am awake and there is a dawn in me."⁶ Morning has already broken for Thoreau, and I repeat: when shall ours come? When shall we be able to embrace, to incorporate youth, Spring, morning, renewal? "We must learn to reawaken and keep ourselves awake, not by mechanical aids, but by an infinite expectation of the dawn, which does not forsake us in our soundest sleep."⁷ The darkest hour is just before dawn; she is always there, an unfailing promise of openness, of pure potentiality, a pregnancy of wisdom, serenity and beauty, a new chance, a new beginning for all those who have apparently failed, who have apparently fallen asleep, who have apparently died by the poison of "cattlelicism."

For those who may despair over the enormity of the task, of one's poor sacramental potential, Thoreau tells us a cautionary myth, a tale about our situation:

> "The life in us is like the water in the river. It may rise this year higher than man has ever known it, and flood the parched uplands; even this may be the eventful year, which will drown out all our muskrats. It was not always dry land where we dwell. I see far inland the banks which the stream anciently washed, before science began to record its freshets. Everyone has heard the story which has gone the rounds of New England, of a strong and beautiful bug which came out of the dry leaf of an old table of apple-tree wood, which had stood in a farmer's kitchen for sixty years, first in Connecticut, and afterward in Massachusetts—from an egg deposited in the living tree many years earlier still, as appeared by counting the annual layers beyond it; which was heard gnawing out for several weeks, hatched perchance by the heat of an urn. Who does not feel his faith in a resurrection and immortality strengthened by hearing of this? Who knows what beautiful and winged life, whose egg has been buried for ages under many concentric layers of woodenness in the dead dry life of society, deposited at first in the alburnum of the green and living tree, which has been gradually converted into the semblance of its well-seasoned tomb,—heard perchance gnawing out

now for years by the astonished family of man, as they sat round the festive board,—may unexpectedly come forth from amidst society's most trivial and handselled furniture, to enjoy its perfect summer life at last! I do not say that John or Jonathan will realize all this; but such is the character of that morrow which mere lapse of time can never make to dawn. The light which puts out our eyes is darkness to us. Only that day dawns to which we are awake. There is more day to dawn. The sun is but a morning star."[8]

Light-everlasting light, even in the middle of the darkest night. The promise of Dawn is always there, the promise of awakening to that infinite light. Even for us, Johns and Jonathans, it is a fascinating prospect, isn't it? As we walk along the narrow footpath of our inaccurately perceived minuscule and pathetic lives, in these dark and frightening woods, it may be worth remembering that one day we shall all, at last, lay our body on Earth, but even then we shall keep playing on Her—Our game—exactly as we are doing today: unconsciously, it is true; but who knows? Maybe we are exactly like that deeply asleep bug, yet perhaps one day we shall also "saunter to the Holy Land, till one day the sun shall shine more brightly than ever he has done, shall perchance shine into our minds and hearts, and light up our whole lives with a great awakening light, as warm and serene and golden as on a bank-side in Autumn."[9]

NOTES

1. Thoreau, H. D. *Journal*. In: Witherell, E. H.; Howarth, W. L.; Sattelmeyer, R.; Blanding, T. (Eds.). *The Writings Of Henry D. Thoreau*. Princeton: Princeton University Press, 1981. V.I., p. 99.
2. Thoreau, H. D. *Journal*. In: Sattelmeyer, R. (Ed.). *The Writings Of Henry D. Thoureau*. Princeton: Princeton University Press, 1984. V.II., p. 78.
3. *Journal*, vol. I, pp. 53–54.
4. *Journal*, vol. I, p. 204.
5. *Idem*, p. 392.
6. Thoreau, H. D. *Walden*, Princeton: Princeton University Press, 1971, p. 90.
7. *Idem, ibidem*.
8. *Idem*, p. 333.
9. *Walking, in* Thoreau, H. D. *Collected Essays And Poems*. The Library Of America, Vol. 124. New York: The Library Of America, 2001, p. 255.

Bibliography

Aeschylus. *The Complete Greek Tragedies*, Vol. 1, *Aeschylus*. Translated and edited by David Greene and Richard Lattimore. Chicago: The University of Chicago Press, 1953.
Aristotle. *The Basic Works of Aristotle*. New York: Modern Library, 2001.
Diogenes Laertius. *Lives Of Eminent Philosophers*, Vol. II. Loeb Classical Library 185. Cambridge, MA: Harvard University Press, 1995.
Emerson, Ralph Waldo. *Essays And Letters*. New York: Library of America, 1983.
Freeman, Kathleen. *Ancilla to the Pre-socratic philosophers*. Cambridge, MA: Harvard University Press, 1996.
Heraclitus. *The Art and Thought of Heraclitus: An Edition of The Fragments with Translation and Commentary*. Cambridge: Cambridge University Press, 1979.
Hölderlin, Friedrich. *Hyperion, or the Hermit in Greece*. Translated by Ross Benjamin. New York: Archipelago, 2008.
Nietzsche, Friedrich. *The Portable Nietzsche*. New York: Viking, 1982.
The Orphic Hymns. Translated by Apostolos N. Athanassakis and Benjamin M. Wolkow. Baltimore: Johns Hopkins University Press, 2013.
Pindar. *Pindar's Victory Songs*, Translated by Frank J. Nisetich. Baltimore: Johns Hopkins University Press, 1980.
Plato. *Complete Works*. Edited by John M. Cooper. Indianapolis, IN: Hackett, 1997.
Seybold, Ethel. *Thoreau: The Quest and The Classics*. New Haven, CT: Yale University Press, 1951.
Spionoza, Baruch. *Spinoza: Complete Works*. Edited by Michael L. Morgan. Translated by Samuel Shirley. Indianapolis, IN: Hackett, 2002.
Thoreau, Henry David. *The Journal of Henry D. Thoreau*. Edited by Bradford Torrey and Francis H. Allen. In Fourteen Volumes Bound as Two. New York: Dover, 1962.
Thoreau, Henry David. *Walden*. Princeton, NJ: Princeton University Press, 1971.
Thoreau, Henry David. *A Week on the Concord and Merrimack Rivers*. Princeton, NJ: Princeton University Press, 1980.

Thoreau, Henry David. "The Writings of Henry David Thoreau." *Journal, Volume 1: 1837-1844*, edited by Witherell, Elizabeth Hall, William L. Howarth, Robert Sattelmeyer, and Thomas Blanding. Princeton, NJ: Princeton University Press, 1981, chap. Journal.

Thoreau, Henry David. "The Writings of Henry David Thoreau." In *Journal, Volume 1: 1837-1844*, edited by Witherell, Elizabeth Hall, William L. Howarth, Robert Sattelmeyer, and Thomas Blanding. Princeton, NJ: Princeton University Press, 1984, chap. Journal.

Thoreau, Henry David. *A Week on the Concord and Merrimack Rivers, Walden, The Maine Woods, and Cape Cod*. New York: Library of America, 1985

Thoreau, Henry David. *Translations*. Edited by Kevin P. Van Anglen. Princeton, NJ: Princeton University Press, 1986.

Thoreau, Henry David. *Collected Essays and Poems*. Library of America, vol. 124, edited by Elizabeth Hall Witherell. New York: Library of America, 2001, chap. *Cep*.

Van Anglen, Kevin P. "Thoreau's Epic Ambitions: 'A Walk to Wachusett' and the Persistence of the Classics in an Age of Science." In *The Call of Classical Literature in the Romantic Age*, edited by Kevin P. Van Anglen and James Engell. Edinburgh, UK: Edinburgh University Press, 2017.

Index

Aeolian harp, 23, 56
Aeschylus, 8, 23–24, 37, 57, 70, 82, 111–12
aesthesis (sensibility), 13
aesthetics, 10, 13–14, 22, 32, 37, 49, 57, 74, 79, 81, 104, 108–9, 116
agriculture, 13–14, 37, 40, 49, 53, 55, 57–59, 62, 65–69, 78
alienation, 14, 21, 37–38, 40, 43, 46, 50, 59–61, 63, 68, 70, 83
Amerindian, 5, 34
anamnesis, 2, 6, 12, 20, 26, 28–29, 42–43, 56, 70, 83, 85–87, 89, 99, 106, 110, 116, 118–19
anthropocentric, 6, 29, 60
Antigone, 44, 115
archaic experience, most, 2, 23, 74, 116
arche (origin, genesis), 4, 7, 11, 28, 48, 58, 81, 85, 118, 123
archeology, 2, 58
architechture, 13–14, 49, 57, 60, 62, 64–66, 68–70, 78
Aristotle, 9–11, 38, 41, 51nn13, 22, 63, 84, 89
attention, 9, 13, 22–23, 41, 50, 57, 63, 80, 87–88, 100–101
authentic, 3, 5, 19, 22–24, 34, 38, 42, 44, 76, 120

awakening, 1–2, 4, 6, 12–13, 15, 22, 25, 38, 41–42, 45, 50, 58, 64, 68, 73, 75, 78, 85–86, 95, 100–105, 107, 113, 116, 120, 126

beauty, 7, 11, 22–24, 31–32, 56, 64, 68, 80, 82–83, 88, 107–8, 110, 113, 115, 118–19, 123, 125
book, 1–3, 5–6, 8, 22, 24, 66, 69, 80–81, 109; book of nature, 80
border, 3, 7, 33, 66, 79, 86, 108, 124; border life with nature, 79
Boston, 40
burrow, 26–27, 29–30, 32–34, 61–62, 64–65

Cape Cod, 22, 33–34
Captain John Brown, 52n34
care/ful, 4, 7, 11, 14–15, 19, 20, 22, 28, 30, 39–41, 62, 64, 80, 83, 87–90, 110, 116
cattle, 42–43, 61, 66, 101
"cattlelicism", 12, 32, 38, 43–44, 61, 101, 125
Christian, 12, 34, 39, 51n22, 59, 73, 84, 114
civilization, 13, 24, 28–30, 32, 37, 48, 53n52, 55, 57, 59, 66, 70, 77, 79–80, 82, 84, 94, 112

colere (to care, to cultivate), 41, 50
community, 9, 26–27, 30–34, 63
Concord, 12, 14, 19–25, 33–35, 38, 40–41, 66, 78, 91, 94, 103
Confucius, 2, 93
conscious/ness, 2, 6, 10, 20–23, 25, 28–31, 37–38, 47, 49, 68, 70, 76, 79, 86, 89, 99, 102–4, 107–9, 114, 117–19, 124
contemplation, 4, 10, 20, 25, 41, 87
Cosmos, 24, 26, 31, 35–36, 73, 83, 113–15, 117, 123
culture, 7–8, 15, 21–22, 29, 31–32, 35, 37–38, 41–42, 48, 50, 55, 57, 65, 70, 73, 78–79, 81–82, 87, 89, 94; culture and nature, 22, 31, 48, 55, 78–79, 81, 92–93

Darwin, Charles, 87
dawn, 3, 8–9, 12–13, 41, 85, 99–101, 103–4, 106–7, 111, 119, 125–26
deformation, 28–29, 33, 59, 61, 67–68; of nature/the landscape, 60, 63, 65, 67, 83–84
deliberation, 47, 62
democracy/tic, 1, 44, 92, 120
determinism, 39, 51n15, 75, 77
domestication, 9, 14, 29, 48–49, 60–61, 65, 67, 77–78, 81–82, 92
dominium, 49, 60–61, 67–68, 92
dwell/ing, 3, 8, 20–21, 23–28, 32–33, 37, 60, 62, 64, 69, 73–75, 91, 125

earth, 2–3, 5–6, 11, 14, 21, 25–27, 43, 56–57, 59, 62, 67–69, 73, 78, 81, 84, 86, 100–101, 107, 109–10, 112–13, 124–26; fidelity to earth, 27
economy/mics, 1, 14, 15, 21, 25–26, 32–33, 35n6, 38, 40, 43, 45, 48, 59, 68, 86, 92, 94, 101–2, 120, 124
Emerson, Ralph W., 12, 21, 31, 39, 42, 50, 80, 88, 114–15
Epicure, 4, 45, 52n44, 76
epistemology/ical, 4, 13, 35n6, 39, 65, 70, 101

ethics/al, 4, 26, 28–30, 33, 36n17, 39–40, 51n15, 63, 71, 87, 125

falsification, 9, 31, 61, 70
fate, 3, 29, 46, 75–76, 78, 95nn4, 11
freedom, 29, 31, 44, 75, 86, 95, 112
free-will, 27, 39, 51n15, 74–75
frontier, 125; frontier life, 79

genealogical, 2, 7–8, 29, 42, 56, 58–59, 66, 73, 85–86, 100, 111
Gnothi sauton (know thyself), 42, 50, 60, 87, 90
God/ess, 4–5, 7, 46–47, 55, 67, 69, 82, 85–86, 90, 94, 104–5, 112–18
Greece, 4, 7–10, 15, 24, 56, 81, 85, 93–94, 100, 108, 111, 114
Greek concepts, 2, 4, 6, 10–12, 26, 31–32, 35n6, 57, 63, 83, 85, 88, 100, 105, 111–11
Greek culture, Thoreau's love of ancient, 7–9, 24, 39, 81, 83, 85, 111–12
Greek language, 24, 26, 63
Greek mythology, 8, 23, 60, 85
Greek philosophy, 10–11, 39, 51, 76
Greek religion, 6, 85, 105
Greek thinkers, 7, 10, 51n13, 73, 81

habitat, 20–21, 24, 26–27, 60, 64, 67, 73
heat, 45–46, 58, 103, 106, 125
Heidegger, Martin, 57
Heraclitus, 50, 53n54, 91, 112, 120
hero/heroic, 8, 12, 24, 37, 43–45, 55–56, 59, 69, 101
history, 1, 3–4, 8–9, 14, 16n16, 24, 30, 55–56, 59–60, 68, 82, 84, 87–88, 111, 116
Hölderlin, 4, 6, 8, 107
Homer, 8, 23–24, 80, 82, 93, 104, 112, 115–16

Iliad, The, 23, 80–81, 112
imperial expansion of the U.S., 1, 34, 40, 44

interdependence, 6–7, 13–14, 21, 23, 27, 33, 49, 65, 73, 75, 79, 88, 93–94, 98, 118, 124
intimacy, 8, 13–15, 20, 28, 33, 59, 79, 83, 86–87, 91, 100, 124

know thyself, 12, 42, 76, 80

landscape, 3, 9, 21, 23–29, 31–35, 49, 57, 60–61, 63, 66–67, 79, 83, 85, 88–89, 91–92
language, 8, 15, 24, 26, 37, 47, 56, 58, 60, 81, 106–7, 112–15, 125
literature, 3, 7, 10, 78, 80–81, 93, 110–12
living according to nature, 4, 50, 58, 76, 95n10, 123
love of nature, 3–4, 8, 79, 86
luxury, 45, 55, 59, 117

machine, 40, 43, 47
Maiden, The, 23, 79, 118–19, 123
Marx, Karl, 45, 61, 93
metaphysics, 5–6, 27, 29–30, 33
method/ology, 7–12, 14, 21, 26, 28, 38, 43, 57–59, 66, 80, 87–88, 100, 124
morning, 2, 8, 24, 55–56, 91, 99–103, 105, 109, 112, 119, 120, 124–26
music, 10, 14, 21, 56, 65, 100–101, 105, 107–9, 113–17
musician, Thoreau as, 19
mystic/ism, 4, 9–10, 19, 112
myth, 3, 7–8, 24, 46, 48, 56, 82, 87, 99, 125
mythology/ical, 3, 7–8, 40, 47, 55, 59, 66, 69–70, 80–81, 112. *See also* Greek mythology
mythopoetic/al language, 8, 37, 55, 80–81, 111

native American, 8, 30, 34, 53n52, 92
natural condition, 6, 29
natural law, 30, 44, 76, 115
natural philosophy, 6, 12, 79, 81, 86–87, 111

nature, 2–7, 9–13, 15, 20, 22–25, 28–32, 34, 37, 41, 44–50, 57–64, 67–70, 73–74, 77–84, 86–87, 89, 91–93, 97–106, 109, 111, 119–20, 123–25; alienation from, 14, 42, 46, 60, 76, 78, 83, 87; and architecture, 14, 57; and beauty, 31–32; as a concept, 75–76; connection to, intercourse with, 15, 23, 31, 37, 76, 79, 87; conscious of herself, 2, 6, 10, 28, 30, 33, 82, 99, 116–17, 124–25; and culture, 73, 78–79, 81; cycles of, 8, 31, 33, 35, 100, 123; deformation of, 29, 48, 64–65, 67–68, 70, 83–84, 120; distance from, our, 6, 38, 42, 47–50, 62, 77–78, 83, 86; divorce from, 29, 32, 42, 73, 84; dominion of/over, 49, 61, 67; falsification of our, 29, 48–49, 60–61, 73; forgotten of herself, 6; God and, 4; and health, 44, 86; humankind as, 4–6, 25, 27, 35; human nature, 27, 29, 39, 47; intimacy with, proximity to, 4, 10, 14, 28, 31, 59, 79, 83–84, 86–87, 91, 100, 112, 124; literature (mythology) and, 8, 23–24; lost connection with, 2, 32, 42, 76; no distinction between, 21, 31; non-duality with, 4, 10, 12–13, 15, 21, 23, 25, 27, 29–30, 32–33, 56, 88, 105–6, 114, 116–17, 123–24; observing/studying herself through us, 28, 79, 82; opposition to, 22, 31; other, as the, 33, 60, 83; and perfection, 114; rational, 76; relationship with, 15, 41, 42, 48–50, 73–74, 76, 78–79, 83, 86, 108, 123–24; and renewal, 94–95, 100; return to, 3, 33; reverence towards, 73; separation from/of, 13, 23, 27, 31–32, 85; to sing, 8, 103, 107, 113–15; and society, 20; "study nature", Emerson, 24, 42, 76; study of, 4, 7, 12, 15, 30, 87, 93; sympathy with, 81, 85; and technique, 37–38; Thoreau as, 103, 108, 118–19;

transformation of, 59–61, 64; violence against, 29, 33–34, 38, 47–48, 60, 63, 83, 93; violent nature, 34–35; we are nature, 43, 48, 50. *See also* we are nature; what is, 70, 73–74, 78, 123

Nietzsche, 3, 27–28, 43, 84, 112

oikeiosis (familiarity), 21, 23
óikos (home, house), 21, 23, 26–27
ontology/ical, 6–7, 27–28, 37, 39, 48–50, 85, 94

paideia (Greek concept of education), 10, 39, 111
panentheism, 4, 6
pedagogue, Thoreau as, 2–3, 19
pedagogy, 2, 7, 10, 13, 15, 25, 50, 74, 85, 88, 112
pedagogy of awakening, 2, 6, 12, 15, 25, 38, 41, 45, 50, 58, 68, 71n26
pedagogy of the wilderness, 15, 75, 78, 82–83, 88, 90, 100
philosopher, 3, 9, 11, 19, 42, 87, 91, 93; Thoreau as, 3, 9, 19, 42
Philosophia Naturalis (Natural Philosophy), 6–7, 65, 115
philosophy, 3, 6, 7, 10–12, 42, 82–83, 87–88, 90, 111–14
philosophy, Greek, 10–11, 39, 51, 86, 89, 112
philosophy as a pedagogy of awakening, 6
philosophy as medicine, 38
physis (nature), 4–6, 81
Pindar, 78, 117
Plato, 9–10, 39, 46, 68, 82, 89, 114–15
poetical meditation, 24
poetry, 3, 7–8, 14, 64, 81–83, 88, 107, 112–13; poetry, Greek, 66, 81; poetry and music, 113, 117; poetry as ontophany, 113; poetry as sacred language, 107; Thoreau's poetry, 3, 8, 14, 20, 64, 87, 107, 121n25

poiesis/praxis (to do, to make), 63–64, 112
political philosophy, 44
politics, 3, 14–15, 19, 21, 26, 31, 33, 38, 40, 43–45, 48, 52n34, 53n52, 57, 59, 63, 68, 78, 82, 84, 86–87, 90, 92–93, 95, 101, 120
Presocratics (archaic thinkers), 4, 7–8, 81–82
Prometheus, 37, 44, 46–47, 49, 52n47, 53n48, 55–57, 59, 70
proximity to the source/nature, 4, 15, 20, 27–28, 79, 86, 92, 108, 112, 116
Pythagoras, 56, 82, 105, 114–15, 117, 121n20

readings of Thoreau, 2–4, 9, 14
religare (reconnect), 3, 28, 79–80
religion, 3–4, 6, 79–80, 112; and nature, 79–80
renaturare (renaturalize), 3, 28
Rousseau, 31, 42, 84

sacramental, 13, 15, 38, 43, 62–64, 100, 121n5, 125; technique, 37–38, 55
science, 6–7, 9, 12, 47, 81–82, 87, 109, 111, 115, 123, 125
sedentism, 13–14, 33, 48–49, 53n52, 59–60, 65
sedes (seat), 64–65
self-knowledge, 12, 30, 63, 76, 78, 83, 87, 90–93. *See also Gnothi sauton*
sincerity, 19, 24
social compact, 31, 44, 84
society, 2, 8, 11–12, 14, 19–21, 30–32, 34–35, 37–45, 52n30, 63, 66, 77–78, 80, 82–83, 88, 92–95, 109, 125
Socrates, 11, 39–40, 57
Sphi(y)nx, 74, 76, 91
Spinoza, 4, 6, 51n15
spring, 8–9, 24, 56, 65, 78, 81, 94, 100, 108, 116, 119, 125
state (political entity), 31, 40, 43–45, 52nn34, 39, 79, 84, 120

Stoic, 4, 6, 35n6, 51nn5, 15, 76, 89, 95n11
sympathy, 22–23, 27, 88, 104, 118; with intelligence, 10–11; with nature, 81, 86–87

technique, 14–15, 37–38, 46–49, 53n5, 55–65, 68–70, 71n6, 83, 108, 117
therapy, 13, 43
Thoreau, Henry. D: as builder, 60–65, 71n13; and Concord, 19–22, 24; and Emerson, 12, 21, 31, 115; on free-will and determinism, 73–75, 77; and the Greeks, 4–14, 21–24, 26, 37, 39, 50n1, 55, 82, 89, 105, 111–17; life, 19–22, 42; as naturalist, 6–7, 12–13; as nature, 23, 29–31, 33–34, 42, 55–56, 75–76, 90–91, 93–94, 102–10, 114–20; as pedagogue, 2, 3, 75; pedagogy, 2–3, 13, 28, 32–33, 39, 41–42, 45, 63, 65, 75–76, 78–81, 83–84, 86–89, 91–95, 99–111, 114–20; as philosopher/thinker, 3, 9–14, 19, 21–22, 37–38, 41–43; philosophy, 4–5, 7, 9–14, 19–24, 30–34, 37–39, 41–43, 48–49, 55–56, 65, 81, 89–95, 99–100, 102–7, 110–14; as poet, 3–5, 14, 102–3, 106–8, 118–20; on self-knowledge, 30, 63, 89–92; on technique, 14, 21, 26, 37, 47–49, 53n51, 57–59, 61–70, 75, 77–78; as tiller, 66–69
Thoreau's critique of society values, 38–45, 48–49, 58–59, 61–66, 68, 77–78, 81, 83–85, 91–93

Thoreau's plastic constitution, 20–22
Thoreau's relationship with culture, 21–22, 31, 55
Thoreau's relationship with nature, 3, 9, 13, 15, 19–23, 27, 29–35, 55–56, 75–88, 92–95, 100–110, 114–20
Thoreau's relationship with society, 19–20, 22, 31, 38–45, 91–92
Thoreau's writings/works, 3, 12, 22, 38
tool, 8, 13–14, 25, 28, 41, 47–49, 58–64, 90
true nature, 29–30, 32, 42, 49, 70, 94, 108, 113
truth, 2, 7, 11–12, 23–24, 43, 56, 64, 74–75, 80, 84, 101, 103, 125

virtue, 80, 85, 88, 95, 113

Walden, 1, 5, 13, 15, 21–24, 30, 33, 38, 41–42, 45, 58, 62, 66, 81, 85, 90–91, 100, 102, 104–5, 108, 110, 118
"we are nature", 3, 6, 10, 50, 78, 87, 117
whole, the, 6–7, 23, 25–26, 28, 32, 68, 79, 82, 99, 103, 118–19, 124
wild, 13, 20, 31–34, 48–49, 66, 73, 76–85, 92–94, 99, 103, 112, 120
wild, being, 15
wildness/wilderness, 14, 25, 29–33, 66, 77–78, 80, 82, 84, 100, 112, 118
wild pedagogy, 75, 82–83, 85, 88, 90
wild thinker, Thoreau as a, 13
wild thought, Thoreau's, 13, 49

Zeus, 46–47, 53n48, 95n11

About the Author

Clodomir B. de Andrade is an associate professor in the Department of Religious Studies at Universidade Federal de Juiz de Fora, Minas Gerais, Brazil, where he has taught over the last eight years. His main philosophical interests and publications are on the non-dualistic traditions of immanence, both in its Eastern avatars (Mahayana Buddhism, Advaita Vedanta and Daoism) as well as in its Western's modulations (Greek religion, Presocratics, Stoicism, Spinoza, Hölderlin, Thoreau). He tries to explore the philosophical possibilities of a naturalistic, immanent, non-metaphysical approach to the relationship between Nature and the sacred. He is also a translator. His current interest is the landscapes of the sacred in Ancient Greece. He is married and lives with his wife and daughter in the High Altitude Atlantic Rain Forest in Mury, Nova Friburgo, near Rio de Janeiro, Brazil.